THE

WISDOM

OF

ANIMALS

THE WISDOM OF ANIMALS

Creatureliness in Early Modern French Spirituality

CATHARINE RANDALL

University of Notre Dame Press   •   Notre Dame, Indiana

Library of Congress Cataloging-in-Publication Data

Randall, Catharine, 1957–
The wisdom of animals : creatureliness in early modern French
spirituality / Catharine Randall.
pages cm
Includes bibliographical references and index.
ISBN 978-0-268-04035-2 (pbk. : alk. paper) — ISBN 0-268-04035-4
(pbk. : alk. paper)
1. Animals—Religious aspects—Christianity. 2. Animals (Philosophy)
3. Montaigne, Michel de, 1533–1592—Criticism and interpretation.
4. Du Bartas, Guillaume de Salluste, seigneur, 1544–1590—Criticism and
interpretation. 5. Bougeant, G.-H. (Guillaume-Hyacinthe), 1690–1743—
Criticism and interpretation. I. Title.
BT746.R36 2014
840.9'362—dc23
2013044486

∞ *The paper in this book meets the guidelines for permanence and durability*
of the Committee on Production Guidelines for Book Longevity
of the Council on Library Resources.

For Henry the horse . . .

Beautiful boy, delight of my eyes, and great teacher

CONTENTS

ACKNOWLEDGMENTS

Infinite gratitude, as always, to my beloved husband, Randall Balmer. Thanks for the great thoughts and enthusiasm from the students in my animal rights classes at both Fordham University and Dartmouth College.

All things come of Thee, O Lord, and of Thine own have we given Thee.

INTRODUCTION

Animals and Authority

The bee . . . gathers its material from the flowers of the garden and of the field, but transforms and digests it by a power of its own. . . . Not unlike this is the true business of philosophy: for it neither relies solely or chiefly on the powers of the mind, nor does it take the matter which it gathers . . . and lay it up in the memory whole, as it finds it, but lays it up in the understanding, altered and digested.

—Francis Bacon, *Novum organum*

Writing about other species . . . has traditionally consoled us by suggesting that "they" are very like us, rather than the other way round. The other way round has always been a problem because it could only be described in human language. . . . The animal kingdom has long been a device for our own self-reflection.

—Andrew Linzey, *Animal Theology*

Work has emerged in the humanities that is challenging the hegemonic position of the human. . . . This work comes under the heading of "animal studies" and its focus . . . tak[es] in not only how humans have lived with animals throughout history, but also how we use animals to think and create.

—Erica Fudge, "Just a Plaything for Your Pet Cat?"

Anima Mundi

Animals have decorated heraldic shields, populated the pages of medieval manuscripts, woven themselves into tapestries, featured as ornamentation on baroque pottery, been formed into the fanciful deformations called gargoyles, farmed our fields, symbolized human weaknesses, lusts, and desires, and insinuated themselves into our hearts. Throughout Western civilization, animals have been our companions, our correctives, and our ciphers as humanity has represented and dealt with issues of authority, cultural strife, and the understanding of ourselves as theological, moral, and social beings. I propose to trace two threads of thought that consistently reappear in early modern texts: how animals are used as a means for humans to explore themselves and the meaning of existence, and how animals can be subjects in their own right with their own minds.

Prior to the Renaissance, narratives often featured animals as symbols of human emotions. The Middle Ages catalogued miscellaneous details and stories about real and imagined animals in bestiaries. Here animals figured the *limitrophe*: the frontiers of things known and unknown, what could be known and what could not be known.

The Middle Ages manifested what has been called a "late-antique medley of Christian allegory and pseudo-science" for its understanding of nature and of animals, relying primarily on a text called the *Physiologus*, a compilation of manuscripts deemed authoritative about animals (Klingender 1971, 341). Many late medieval texts about animals organized their suppositions and arguments around proofs drawn from the *Physiologus*. During the twelfth and thirteenth centuries, the *Physiologus* was rewritten as the popular medieval *Bestiarium*, "the earliest medieval picture book devoted entirely to animals," which greatly contributed to the Carolingian revival of natural science in particular (Klingender 1971, 342). Animal symbolism closely linked with the sciences was perceived, and codified, as cultural convention.[1] This was a very fertile period for the production of a variety of imaginative literary works concerned with animals,[2] and often animals supplied both the format and the impetus for authorship.

The medieval period also looked to Aristotle's *History of Animals*, Virgil, Pliny, and other classical writers as sources of information about animal life. Preachers consulted collections of animal stories in Latin for exempla that they could use in their sermons. Compiled during the thirteenth and fourteenth centuries, such compendia were now also read by lay people and used in secular, vernacular works of fiction.

The illustrations in medieval manuscripts in virtually every genre also referenced anecdotes about animal life and sometimes expressed a perception of animals that was more naturalistic than stereotyped and subordinated to didactic aims.[3] Further, heraldic art began to incorporate animals systematically, drawing on the stock of symbolic meanings ascribed to members of the animal kingdom. Birds and animals became prevalent, significant features, often providing the visual component in the self-mythologizing of the individual or family represented.

During the late fourteenth and early fifteenth centuries, people began to make detailed observations from life about the ways animals lived, their habits and customs, and to add this new awareness to the symbolic cultural associations already formed. For example, Jacopus de Voragine's *Légende dorée* shows many lifelike and naturalistic— but also anthropomorphized—actions of animals, as does Ugolino da Santa Maria's *Actus Beati Francisci* with its tale of St. Francis and the wolf of Gubbio. In such stories, the animals encapsulate a preachment but also provide occasional comic relief and a firm experiential footing in the real world, with the intent of encouraging the devout reader to envision the saint performing his spiritual and miraculous actions in the knowable arena of daily life. Narrative applications of *animalia* flourished during this time.[4]

The natural authority that animals embodied came to be construed as a necessary starting point of lessons that humans should strive to incorporate and to surpass.[5] In this respect and others, the Renaissance initiated a great paradigm shift. Intricately rendered, true-to-life artistic representations of animals, such as Pisanello's *Head of a Horse*, epitomize this period. Renaissance thinkers asked questions such as whether humans could ever know what went on in an animal's mind, or whether an animal could comprehend what went on in a human mind. The Renaissance viewed animals primarily in two ways: in their reality sui generis, and as *magistri*, or teachers. Animals possessed wisdom and knowledge surpassing that of man, but from which man could draw, through *imitatio* and *innutritio*, the normative methods for treating authoritative sources. Man could learn from the animal kingdom. Animals also represented the state of the world as sixteenth-century writers and authors perceived it.[6]

Disturbing phenomena of war or sin or crime could be described through recourse to animal metaphors (Hale 1994, 63). In the fraught context of the Wars of Religion, the disappearance of a high moral assessment of humanity, of the possibility of ethical decision making, of truthful action and compassionate treatment of one's fellows, occasioned reflection on how to represent man to himself.[7] With the human no longer able to offer an estimable standard or norm, writers turned to animals to express their concerns about human nature as they were experiencing it.[8]

Animals thus provided a tool for thinking about a profoundly negative alteration in the human condition (*Homo homini lupus*). Animals also became the teachers for how to recuperate once-admired human traits that now seemed to be in danger of disappearing. If man was a wolf to his neighbor, the notion of "wolf" had become contaminated by the human, rather than exalted through association, and needed to be retrieved and rehabilitated to conform to the wolf's natural characteristics rather than to the abusive connotations forced upon the animal. Animals could then illustrate, in every sense of the word, how human nature should be and how it might be restored. At the same time, animals could re-become their animal selves. Early modern writers began to explore the animal imagery that they often used in their writing.

Some Thoughts about Theory

In many varied and interdisciplinary ways during the Renaissance, a new interest in the relations between animals and humanity developed in the examination and illustration of the comparative anatomy of man and animals, as well as the comparison of the perceived ethics of animal and human societies. This interest led to a radical change in the rhetoric and style used to talk about animals and humans. During the Renaissance the natural world often served as a vehicle to delineate and test out the unknown, what was unfamiliar: animals became a vehicle for knowing, part of a process, rather than an imposed, static *summum* of the already known (Hale 1994, 529).

And what was already known was, in large part—as this was the dominant discourse of the age—theological. The debate as to whether animals have been simply put on earth for our use or whether we owe them certain dignity and rights is long-standing, and each of the authors in this study had to situate himself in reference to this theological issue.[9]

The prevailing view during the early modern era is that of Roman Catholic theology as explicated by Thomas Aquinas. St. Thomas in the *Summa theologica* (II-II, q. 64, art. 1) asserts that it is morally and theologically acceptable to use or to kill animals, as they "have no sense . . . [and are] irrational" creatures (Aquinas 2004, 124). Animals in the divine scheme of things "are subject to our use" (*Summa theologica* II-II, q. 64, art. 1; Aquinas 2004, 124). They therefore do not possess natural rights. Although Aquinas allows that all of creation is essentially good, the realm in which justice and charity—indeed, salvation—are operative is very circumscribed. And nonhuman creatures are excluded. This has been the prevailing doctrinal position in the West since the thirteenth century. And although Augustine introduced the notion of a *sensus interior* that he discerned in animals as well as in humans (*De libero arbitrio* 2.8–10), this was not enough to alter the prevailing Thomist theological position.

While in the medieval era and early Renaissance animals had at least been construed as possessing wisdom of which man could avail himself, by the seventeenth century many thinkers, having exalted human authority, reverted to an earlier Thomistic notion that animals were brute material to be shaped by humanity. The *sapience* that Renaissance writers had discerned in animal life was now to be corrected and reshaped by superior human intellect. Hence the term *dressage* for the training of horses, for instance: the implication of *dresser* being that we discipline, mold, and train them and that they have nothing to teach us.[10] Even more dismissive was René Descartes's view that animals were merely another form of automata, animated machines that felt no emotion. He maintained that a live dog, flayed to the bone, that cried and squealed was merely an assemblage of parts. A dog could not think, therefore it was not.[11]

Much work has been done recently to dismantle such positions; the Episcopal priest and animal rights activist Andrew Linzey goes back to the "beginning" in terms of Western Christian thought on animals. He argues that Aquinas's position is neither "quite Christian nor scriptural enough" but rather amounts to a truncated misreading (1995, 18). In *Animal Theology*, Linzey argues most compellingly from a solidly "orthodox" Christian perspective for the extension of the redeeming power of the Incarnation to all of creation. He critiques the Aristotelian views of Aquinas, who places humans, as superior and as the sole recipients of redemption, over and against animals, lesser elements of creation intended for human use.[12] This would imply that part of creation had no theological relevance or application. Linzey, however, asserts that all of creation is to be taken up equally into redemption and that man's attitude toward creatures should imitate that of the Suffering Servant Christ.[13] The suffering of animals should be alleviated through humans as agents of God, and animals should be "liberated" from the "groaning of creation" through an ethics of "generosity" rather than treated according to a utilitarian self-interest.[14]

Linzey takes on other theologians as well,[15] criticizing John Calvin for a "selective biblical literalism" that enables him to assert man's superiority over the creatures (this will be relevant for the Protestant poetics of Guillaume Salluste Du Bartas, discussed in chapter 2).[16] Further, Linzey affiliates himself with Brian Horne and Keith Ward, who construct theological arguments for the existence of animal souls (an important component of Bougeant's argument) (Linzey 1994, 98–100).[17]

Other scholars in animal rights and animal studies—early and influential among them Keith Thomas in his *Man and the Natural World* (1983)—probe how animals are used in texts and offer helpful insights with which I have engaged in this book. They rightly ask whether experimental, or other, use of animals is ethically justifiable. They suggest that animals should no longer be construed as "lenses" or constructed as media through which to view humans and should instead be acknowledged to have value and legitimacy in their own right.[18] Donald, for example, has argued that "where animals are the ostensible subject of a work of literature, it has been too easy to interpret them simply as symbols or metaphors for aspects of the human: to such an extent that animals themselves appear to have no existence or meaning, other than those conferred on them by writers. . . . Seldom has the representation of animals *per se* been thought worthy" (2007, vi). Nor has man been interrogated for what he seeks to say through *animalia*, so that the resulting distortions can be revealed.

Diana Donald sums up the current critical state of affairs in her study of eighteenth-century animal art in England: "What is remarkable is . . . the absence of a conceptual framework within which the disparity [in impressions of animals within our contemporary culture] c[an] be observed. The part played by animals in the history and culture of the western world has only recently begun to attain the status of a distinct, substantive field of study. It has yet to . . . establish a methodology through which human-animal relations in western history would be illuminated" (2007, vi).

The early modernist Erica Fudge shows how the presence of animals in early modern texts may raise questions and concerns about how humanity has claimed omniscience. She argues that, in fact, animals enact curtailments of man's ability to know. Animal rights, like the rights of African Americans, women, and other groups in earlier centuries, have been neglected because their existence calls assertions of hegemony into question. Fudge asserts that "putting animals at the heart of cultural change rather than presenting them as mere passive objects of human work challenges assumptions about who and what can be considered the moving forces of culture" (2002a, 1). She suggests that perceptions of animal rationality—however that might be construed—as instinct, communicability, sociability, language, a rationality that parallels but differs from ours—may have much to tell us about how we construct them and how we construct ourselves.

Donna Haraway's groundbreaking *Primate Visions* dismantles "humanist" approaches to animals, showing how we really are representing ourselves when we claim to be studying animals (1989, 3). Perhaps even more compelling is the perspective she develops in *When Species Meet*, where she argues for giving animals rights as subjects of their own lives rather than as objects of our pity (2008, 30). We need to move beyond the position where animals occupy the position of alterity.

We return to the work of Andrew Linzey, inevitably and helpfully, for his position is perhaps the most important for the arguments advanced in this volume. Linzey develops what he calls "animal theology" and, in so doing, does much of the theoretical groundwork necessary for anyone who finds it textually and contextually necessary to work within a Western theological tradition. This book works toward what I term "a theology of creatureliness," the primary distinction from Linzey's "animal theology" being my focus on humans' viewing of animals—whether by dominant gaze or by participation in a natural phenomenon—and an emphasis, common to the authors examined in this study, on an animal's activity as quintessentially representative of its essence.

"Theo-logos" is a "God Word," and each of the authors whom I discuss displays that "God Word" in his own way, attempting to elucidate what it has to say, and how it interacts, with *animalia*. In the case of St. François de Sales, for instance, the theology of creatureliness uses animal activities as patterns of natural knowledge that humans can imitate to arrive at a deeper spiritual perspective. De Sales does not use this knowledge to dominate animals, and he does not distort the pattern of animal experience and knowing—that is the issue of authority with which Bougeant has to deal—rather, he respects and reveres the animal's nature as revealing something of God, in a movement toward a holistic apprehension of the divine in the natural world. Through the creature and our own creatureliness we enter into relationship with the Creator, and as Linzey points out, through our creaturely commonality we finally begin to glimpse the extent and significance of our interconnectedness.

The Fauna of Faith

The aim of this volume is to elucidate in an interdisciplinary way the early modern perspective on animals and the ways in which animals are applied to affirm, alter, or oppose authority, whether social, cultural, literary, or, especially, theological. I examine the multitude of references to animals in various early modern texts and analyze each author's uses of such references and his relationship to the animal kingdom. I explore the role and significance of animals in the narrative: Which animals are selected, and what factors motivate their inclusion? Where are they featured, and how are the animal references used in the text? How do they inflect textual development? How do they influence the text's relationship to authority, tradition, orthodoxy, and creativity?

The early modern period is often viewed as having been the crucible of sixteenth-century protoscientific thought, with a consequent influence on poetic and prose development regarding animal life, so that it is especially suited to an examination of the presence and problematics of *animalia* for the writing project. Each chapter offers an assortment of perspectives on animals or a debate about an issue regarding them from a particular historical moment within that period. The chapters are framed using sensory, often synesthetic referents, as this is a book about animals and the world they inhabit and enrich. Such framing is further appropriate given the new tendency to spiritualize the world of the senses after the Wars of Religion and the Council of Trent: the time period of, or the period that would later influence, the texts examined in this study. Probably the most consistent referent is the sense of sight, with all that it entails: ocular domination, visive violence, a will to spectate, the production of theatrical spectacle, viewed gestural language.[19] Sight is also, relentlessly, situated within theological discourse: an omniscient God surveying his creation features prominently in Du Bartas's work, for example.

In the first chapter, Montaigne, along with, to some extent Ronsard, Noël Du Fail, and others, offers a panoply of positions concerning animals and authority as they were construed in the sixteenth century. Montaigne argues that the perceived difference of humanity from other creatures is a misperception: in fact, the difference between one man and another may be greater than that between any individual and a particular animal. Montaigne's theriophily leads him to conclude that animal "stupidity"—as we so call it—often far surpasses the capabilities of our own intelligence. Montaigne further develops the understanding of animals' instinctual noetic ability, which contrasts with flawed and limited human reason. He admires animal knowledge and experience and uses animal knowing as a rationale for religious toleration. Animals' structures—notably, the swallows' *contexture*, their nest—he makes emblematic of his own text. Primarily in the "Apologie pour Raimond Sebond," Montaigne elucidates a position in which animals enact a hermeneutics derived from and displayed from nature, one that humans would do well to emulate. He portrays animals as morally superior to men and notes that they have been our great teachers.[20] Not only does he often use animal imagery and references to the natural world, but he also makes those allusions as accurate as early modern protoscience permits and draws on his own experience and observation. The descriptions of animal life in the *Essais* (1580) offer ways to construe "what is in here": the inner man, the self, a Renaissance construction, can be known in comparison to, and in contrast with, "animal nature."[21]

The second chapter, on the Calvinist poet Du Bartas, presents his viewpoint on animals as an early modern version—with some nuances—of what we today call "dominion theory." It is striking how dissimilar the use of animal imagery among sixteenth-century Calvinists is from its application by early modern Catholics. Calvin's distrust of the world and its lures seems to have been profound; in *Institutions de la religion chrétienne*, his treatise on Protestant doctrine and ecclesiology, he rarely employs an animal metaphor.[22] Du Bartas follows in the Protestant path epitomized by Calvinist writers, who viewed nature as fallen and therefore in need of restitution. Holding to a providential focus and developing a theological anthropology, Du Bartas explicates biblical literature, including wisdom literature, and frequently draws on biblical references to the natural world, such as those in Proverbs and the Book of Job, in his own works.[23] In his encyclopedic compendium of animals in verse, *La sepmaine* (1578), the animals described are less important than the use of their collection to reinforce the mastery of the Creator, epitomized by a global, dominating gaze. This Protestant epic poem praises the wonders of creation, evokes animals prior to the Fall, and uses them as ciphers that merely indicate what man once knew but, through his sin, has forgotten or lost access to. Du Bartas's treatment of animals, consequently, is usually characterized by a theological inquiry into the twinned issues of authority and authorship (Hale 1994, 560).

Montaigne's work with animal metaphors and Du Bartas's catalogue of creatures exemplify a willingness, in the early modern
period, to think about the place of animals in the natural order and to
consider humans' embeddedness in the natural world. Animals, in
this era, featured as *vehicles for knowing.*

As Protestantism and Catholicism diverged, so did their theologies with regard to nature and especially animals. The third chapter
describes the development and antecedents of the new genre of the
devotional manual and its use of animals.[24] It also contrasts the primary text of the chapter, the *Introduction à la vie dévote* (1609) by St.
François de Sales, to texts of devotional literature such as those of
John Donne and St. John of the Cross, in order to show de Sales's
innovations. Some reference is also made to de Sales's continuators
and emulators, primarily Jesuits,[25] attesting to the persistence and
effectiveness of de Sales's new paradigm. De Sales is an important
example of an early modern figure who reads animals as intimate
"others": they differ from us; they have a path to indicate to us; their
difference from us is a mark of being earthly yet unmarked by sin.
By contemplating their activities, man can raise himself to a higher
awareness of the sense of both his earthly and his spiritual existence.
"By their very 'otherness,' [animals] help us define ourselves."[26] De
Sales's popular and widely consulted manual relies heavily on animal imagery to suggest different modes for being in God's presence.
While Montaigne and Du Bartas have been explored already in terms
of their use of animalisms, de Sales—and those influenced by him—
have never been examined in such a way, perhaps because their genre
is the devotional manual, and the critical approach to such literature
has generally been either to implement practically or to elucidate theo-
retically its meditational method. Devotional literature—construed
as para-ecclesial—apparently was allowed more doctrinal latitude
and liberty from ecclesiastical censorship as well. A new avenue of
interpretation opens up through the focus of an analytical lens on
what has until now been construed as the province of prayer. De Sales
delineates and exemplifies a theology of creatureliness that emphasizes the characteristic activities of animals, rather than their classifi-
able attributes, and analogizes them to recommended states of mind,
feelings, and actions, as well as spiritual possibilities for the believer.

The seventeenth century shows a paradigm shift: some thinkers react to the Cartesian reduction of animals to the status of soulless "machines," and predominantly Roman Catholic writers begin to refer to *animalia* as, in a way, *machines à penser*—usually spiritualized in intent and application. Animals are valued; they pose as vehicles for *our* knowing. Animals become not only familiar fauna but also intimate companions of the soul, even *familiars* of the spiritual seeker, and then subjects in their own right.

There is also a separation of ways within Roman Catholicism itself: a paradigm split, perhaps. Increasingly, not the doctrinal texts, but rather the *spiritual literature*—generically less confined by dogma, more open to personalistic expressions of belief—expresses a holistic environmental and noetic unity and a shared *anima* between humans and animals. And, paradoxically, animal references become more numerous and more contested in Catholic writings as the era of scientific certainty progresses. Le père Bougeant's *Amusement philosophique sur le langage des bêtes* (1730), written outside religious genres altogether as a piece of philosophical speculation and showmanship for a salon audience, is nevertheless condemned as heretical, while de Sales's spiritual manual from a century earlier, though in some ways also skirting heresy, passes unimpeded.

The fourth chapter, on le père Bougeant's *Amusement*, a text that has received little critical attention but that has nonetheless earned its author something of a cult following among animal rights activists today, incorporates some of the criticism leveled at him by authorities, as well as showing how his assertion that animals possess language and even souls prefigures findings in current animal theories.[27] Bougeant's wildly popular book, intended for an audience similar to that of Jean de La Fontaine, whose defense of animals in his "Discours à Madame de la Sablière" is also examined in this chapter, posits a reciprocal fondness on the part of animals for us and affirms that animals possess a form of language that, while different from ours, has value and coherence for them as well as for us (Bougeant 1739/1954, 10; Phillips 2002, 3). While La Fontaine anthropomorphizes and attempts to fight Cartesianism through storytelling, Bougeant asserts a valuable difference between man and animal, one based on instinct, experience, and observation—especially of animal communication. Although he ostensibly writes as a popularizer and for a salon audience, he couches his arguments in traditional theological language. Much of Bougeant's reasoning shows affinities with Montaigne's theriophilic perspective, but Bougeant pushes much further, to his daring assertion that animals possess souls. The *Amusement* was condemned by the Vatican for this heretical speculation influenced by Eastern ideas of metempsychosis; Bougeant was briefly exiled as a result and was required to publish an apology and a retraction of his assertions. Bougeant's text thus led to a confrontation involving animals and authority, with the Catholic *magisterium* deeming Bougeant's arguments dangerous to the faith.

Early modern philosophical texts (Montaigne) and theological texts, both Protestant (Du Bartas) and Roman Catholic (de Sales and Bougeant), all display ways of instrumentalizing animals that reflect particular ideologies and worldviews. Their treatment of animals shows a rich complexity and synesthetically evokes animal existence. Perspectives range from dominion theology to an appreciation of animal instinct and experience, a cooperation with animals in the new genre of devotional literature, and even a compelling argument for the existence of souls. A theology of creatureliness develops during this period, displayed not only in texts but also in other cultural productions, offering new avenues for relationships among animals, man, and God.

SIXTEENTH-CENTURY ANIMAL AVATARS IN MONTAIGNE AND HIS CONTEMPORARIES

When I play with my cat, who can say whether she is playing with me, or whether I am playing with her?
—Michel de Montaigne, "Apology for Raimond Sebond"

No, no, my cat that looks at me in my bedroom or in the bathroom, this cat . . . does not appear here as representative, or ambassador, carrying the immense symbolic responsibility with which our culture has always charged the feline race. . . . If I say, "It is a real cat" that sees me naked, it is in order to mark its unsubstitutable singularity. . . . It comes to me as this irreplaceable living being that one day enters my space, enters this place where it can encounter me, see me, even see me naked. Nothing can ever take away from me the certainty that what we have here is an existence that refuses to be conceptualized.
—Jacques Derrida, *The Animal That Therefore I Am*

The Wisdom of Solomon and the "Science" of a Swallow: Montaigne on Animals

Montaigne's famous interaction with his cat provides the reader with a ludic spectacle, as well as giving Montaigne himself a philosophical framework from which to approach the nature of animality and the twinned questions of animal consciousness and language. The micronarrative relies on the sense of sight but also uses imagination coupled with logical deduction to interrogate the issue. Further, the notion of mirror image or specularity, the doubling of the cat's curiosity about the man with the man's question about the cat, underscores the relationship—even the equality—between the two. Creatureliness seems no impediment to this thoughtful feline.

> Montaigne was willing to . . . take seriously the claims of ancient philosophers and natural historians that animals could talk. . . . According to Montaigne, animals . . . communicate with humans by their calls and gestures. They use sign language. . . . Their behavior displays complex reasoning; they weep, like humans. The most important emotions and feelings in humans and animals cannot be adequately expressed in words. . . . Montaigne's phenomenology of speech includes all of these kinds of signifying. It is an activity shared by humans and animals: "Qu'est-ce que parler?" (Senior 1997, 67)

But creatureliness seems to have posed an impediment to Montaigne, in that he avoids asking what the cat's response might mean. At least he does not anthropomorphize. Yet he does not consider an alternative mode of interaction either, one that would "[risk] knowing something more about cats and *how to look back*."[1]

Montaigne's use of animals in the *Essais*, and particularly his use of them in the "Apologie pour Raimond Sebond," sets the stage for the two differing strands of animal application and interpretation in the seventeenth century that are examined later in this book, both theological: the Protestant (epitomized by the Calvinist poet Guillaume Salluste Du Bartas) and the Catholic (represented by St. François de Sales and the Jesuit Guillaume-Hyacinthe Bougeant). While Montaigne's references are not always theological, some are, and these will be picked up and developed divergently by later writers who build on his philosophical insights in more specifically spiritual ways.

Cranes and gnats, swallows and cats, migrating birds and swallows in a barnyard, horses, lapdogs and hunting dogs, bees and silkworms, maggots—animal life and insect species throng and swarm and entwine their forms around and through Montaigne's *Essais*. Sometimes they feature in proverblike utterances, encapsulations of "received wisdom"; at other times they appear to embody Montaigne himself, or the workings of his intellect—how he pillages other authorities and scavenges them for quotations, for example. The word *comme* (like, as) predominates, as Montaigne draws equations of similarity and lines of difference between animals and humans;

comparison brings the animal kingdom into relation with the human world of knowing.

In portraying animals, Montaigne invariably represents their instinctual ability to know, as contrasted with the ultimately flawed and inadequate human capacity to attain full understanding. Montaigne's self-chosen *devise*, the balance or scale, features in his writing and is contrasted with the certain and instinctual knowledge of animals. His own ability to know is unsteady and unbalanced ("My scales are uneven and unreliable; what assurance do I have that I am right this time, as opposed to others?") because it relies on intellect rather than instinct.[2] So Montaigne writes himself into his own endeavor, comparing his capacity for knowledge to that of animals, birds, and insects and coming up short. His "Apologie" expresses a valuing of instinct over reason, context over disembodied thought, experience over intellect or ratiocination: "Swallows, which we see upon their return in the spring ferreting about in every corner of our houses, are they looking with no judgment and seeking out in a thousand places without discernment the most appropriate in which to lodge? And in this beautiful and remarkable interweaving ["contexture"] of their structures, is it possible that these birds use a square rather than a round shape, an obtuse angle rather than a right angle, without knowing the circumstances and what will result [from these choices]?"[3]

The swallows' "jugement" and "discrétion" are not cerebral constructs, obviously, but rather a lived and unreflective wisdom granted by nature and born of instinct, an intuitive knowing that defies and surpasses, even obviates, intellectual knowing. And the result is a beautiful creation, a "belle et admirable contexture"—the nests they build, a wrapping-round of twigs and leaves, with mud as mortar, in the best place possible, the safest perch to be found.

To such a state of non-self-aware, unratiocinated cognition Montaigne aspires. He hopes his *Essais*, with its composite structure nested around thoughts and studded with bits and pieces of authorities secreted away, like a magpie's treasure trove of bright and shiny objects, will produce a web, a concatenation, a *toile* (perhaps, even, a proto-Internet) epitomizing interrelationships and cross-references. In fact, Montaigne describes birds' nest making and spiders' web making similarly: "Why does the spider weave a web in one place and neglect another site? Why does it use, this time, one kind of knot, another time another kind, if the spider lacks deliberation, thought, and the ability to decide?" Implicitly, the web seems to be a metaphor for the embodied and instinctual foundation for his own knowing (Randall 2000).[4] Just as the swallows build their nests in the framework of old buildings and barns, Montaigne purports to shelter his thoughts within the *Essais*'s textual structure.[5]

In so doing, Montaigne speaks of many animals, among them the silkworm and the bee, to name only a few.[6] However, the *hirondelle* or swallow holds a particularly privileged place in the *Essais*. The swallow's nest is a cunning *contexture:* a metaphor for textuality. Montaigne's *Essais*, so rich in meditation on the human condition, are as yet mostly unmined for how animal nature precedes, coexists with, and influences (or provides a parallel existence to and sometimes a critique of) the human experience. Montaigne's interest in Stoicism led him to speculate, and probably to believe, that animals had souls (Navarro-Reyes 2010, 259). This conjecture prompted him to take very seriously the sorts of societies, such as anthills and associations of crows, in which animals existed. He then juxtaposed these entities and interactions productively (and sometimes provocatively) with man's cultures. The cultural relativism for which Montaigne is so famous, such as that to which the essay "Des cannibales" attests, pleads the case for aboriginal cultures having something equally as good as, if not better than, European cultures (Handler 1986, 23). Montaigne takes such argumentation a step further, often constructing the case that animal nature is far superior in many ways to human and possesses an innate and natural authority and rectitude that man would do well to emulate.[7]

Montaigne, like Socrates, strove to "put philosophy within the reach of everyman and the daily life of ordinary people."[8] To realize this realistic and pragmatic purpose, he deliberately chose metaphors and references drawn from quotidian and creaturely existence: in "On Physiognomy" he approvingly says that Socrates "speaks of nothing more than coachmen, carpenters, shoemakers, and masons," and, we might add, animals.[9] Montaigne's signature style reflects this organicity and preoccupation with flesh-and-blood existence and comparisons: he alludes to it as "a style of flesh and bone."[10]

Thus, for instance, in attempting to describe a sound pedagogical method, Montaigne finds it useful to refer to equitation, the art of riding, speaking metaphorically of how the teacher should set the pupil "on his horse" and "get him trotting."[11] The pedagogue introduces a concept, then encourages the student to apply it—first to mount the horse and then to trot. Montaigne brings in more animal allusions by stipulating that he does not want students to become "donkeys burdened with books" and stating his abhorrence for rote learning, which he compares to the force-feeding of geese.[12] On another occasion, explaining why he has decided to withdraw from public life and hole up in his library, Montaigne compares himself to a turtle retreating into its shell.[13] Many, many times, Montaigne displays human nature as equivalent to, or at least very much like, that of the animal kingdom; we cling to life as an animal does to its prey, "tooth and nail," he notes.[14] So the customary literary authorities with which contemporary authors stuff their pages are not always as essential to Montaigne's textual development—despite his fondness for classical citation and the inscriptions on his library walls—as are animal models of experience and sensory processing. Animal avatars or archetypes—in the sense that for Montaigne they embody qualities and philosophic concepts—offer a new mode for developing authority. This is a lived, experiential, instinctual, undeniable authority.[15]

Especially in the "Apologie" Montaigne moves beyond the issue of how, or how perfectly or imperfectly, we may know to suggest that by reflecting on and observing animal knowing we can devise a process or strategy for our own alternative knowing. The swallow's knitting together of a nest, its flight to the four corners of the globe, its ferreting about in the four corners of our chambers, and its skimming of the confines of each corner with its L-shaped tail, like avian calipers, suggest ways for human beings to gain knowledge, link experience and reason, construct scenarios for understanding, and establish a frame that both protects and delimits knowledge.

Often taken as his seminal essay that describes and enacts his way of working with and responding to authority and authorities,

Montaigne's "Apologie pour Raimond Sebond" squarely identifies nature and natural experience as the primary and privileged mode of knowing, even when nature can itself be shown to be not entirely reliable (Pouilloux 1995, 20). Montaigne further values the natural order by moving away from an explicitly religious framework when he calls God the architect of the natural order, rather than the Supreme Being.

Montaigne's method throughout the essays, and especially here, is to compensate for the limitations to man's comprehension by providing images that evoke and concretize concepts. Raimond Sebond, the ostensible subject of the *essai* and Montaigne's pretext for developing a description of his own style and methodology through the extended discussion of noetics and nest building, had sought to compel humanity to act on behalf of all creatures—more a "dominion" model of human and animal interaction. Montaigne, however, insists instead on the similarities and, therefore, the intimate links between man and other creatures. The relationship for him is horizontal rather than vertical. "We owe justice to humans, and grace and compassion to other creatures. . . . There is some interchange between us and them, and a certain mutual obligation."[16]

Swallows are instinctual creatures. They are known to be "homing" birds; they return every spring to the same place and, indeed, to the same structure they have previously built if it is still extant (and, today, swallows are legally protected, as are their nests; it is forbidden by law to remove the nest once building has begun). Montaigne selects the swallow to epitomize the concept of the instinctual basis for certainty that such creatures possess. He underscores humanity's incomprehension of this innate ability by placing question marks at the end of the first two sentences of the passage on swallows quoted above ("Are they looking with no judgment and seeking out in a thousand places without discernment . . . ? . . . Is it possible that these birds use a square rather than a round shape . . . without knowing the circumstances and what will result?"). The question marks represent typographically man's incredulity: it seems impossible that these birds can possess such vast, varied, and reliable knowledge. Indeed, the foregoing section of the "Apologie" was devoted to demonstrating how little man could know for certain, and also to effecting new "ouvertures," apertures and spaces for new ways of conceiving both man's rational limits and what might lie beyond.[17] Now, by invoking the swallow's certainty, Montaigne launches a hermeneutic discussion: What can we know? How do we know what we know? Is the knowledge that other creatures possess superior to ours? If so, should we not scale back our arrogance accordingly? We need to become more like the animals in order to know more, Montaigne daringly avers: "We must make ourselves beasts in order to become wise," and "Has God not made beastlike all the [human] knowledge of this world?"[18] Animals feature as a disregarded kingdom that Montaigne seeks to rehabilitate and emulate: "animals . . . earth-dwellers, our countrymen."[19]

Tom Conley has argued that the figure of the swallows serves to show that knowledge must occur within context; just as the swallows construct their nest within the four corners of a barn, for instance, so too must knowledge be pinned to known frameworks (1992; 2011, 13). Because swallows represent for Montaigne the workings of human comprehension derived from nature and from experience, they also represent those boundaries beyond which such knowledge may not go. Conley concludes that "the swallow never returns to the end of the essay to assure the order of a seasonal continuity that would guarantee the order of God and Christian faith" (1998, 936).

Swallows are emblems of Montaigne's hermeneutic project. He wants to embody the soaring flight of human conjecture, at the same time as he pins to four walls our ability to know: even liminal capacity possesses limits; there is a *beyond* we cannot attain. There is an authority that surpasses ours. But is that authority God? Or, is it, rather, nature, seen as autonomous of its creator, "une singuliere science" evidenced by animals? (Montaigne 1924, 2:479).

The latter is more likely, especially since swallows *do* in fact return elsewhere in Montaigne's writing—along with numerous other evocations of various nesting birds, as representative of the beginnings of an argument for religious toleration.[20] It would appear that in the "Apologie" Montaigne deliberately strives to move away from former theological "certainties" and instead to survey in a positive light different systems of knowing by exploring plural theologies and applying diverse hermeneutic paths. The swallows, so minute and, yes, so flighty, are the equivalent of the cannibals favorably mentioned in "Des cannibales," who, even if they are not wearing European breeches, and are judged as savage and stupid by the Europeans for this omission, seem truly to have more compassion and more tolerance than their Western counterparts. Wild is privileged over civilized in that essay, just as nature and instinct trump rationalistic schemas in this one. What works best, Montaigne finds after his examination of the swallows and other members of the animal kingdom—storks and ants—is *juste mesure*, aptness, utility, and tried-and-true experience, and he deduces these lessons and recommends them to his fellow men: "We have no more need for offices, for rules and laws of conduct in our [human] community than cranes or ants do in theirs. And nonetheless we see that they live their lives in a very orderly way, even without such erudition. If man were wise, he would take each thing into consideration from the perspective of whether it was the most useful and best suited to his life."[21]

Writing during the Wars of Religion, Montaigne refers to the devastations of civil strife. Since he is describing builder birds, he evokes buildings, but these are structures of another sort: the buildings designed to harbor faith: "The [swallows' structures] caused him to remember the nests that sparrows and crows had been going about France hanging from the vaults and walls of churches that Huguenots had recently destroyed."[22] Careful not to take sides, scrupulous to espouse neither Catholic nor Calvinist cause, Montaigne uses the images of sparrows and crows nesting in the ruined rafters of torn-down churches to show that nature will recuperate these structures for her own purposes. From what has been left a remnant, a new beginning emerges: "building and un-building [*desbastiment*]. . . . What a pattern, what a model!"[23] The structures of theological controversy and spiritual strife are appropriated for natural—and much more benign—ends, and the scaffolding on which belief had reposed, now unsteady and worthless to man, provides an acceptable support for the continuation of the natural order. The deleterious attempt to destroy the housing of another's religious faith is now circumvented; the ideological freight has been removed, and space has been cleared for nature and instinct—for Montaigne, the definition of true know-ing, without prejudice or preconception—to take over.

The essay contains no simplistic or naive valorizing of innocent animals over depraved or deficient humanity. Nature abounds with structures built by creatures other than man.[24] This "animal architec-ture," as it has been called, is in many ways far superior to the struc-tures that man makes—as well as to the intellectual structures he erects for himself, which harbor only the illusion of certainty, in many cases. The fact that reason does not appear to be involved, or does not need to be involved, in animals' structuring activity is actually an asset: "Leave nature alone; she understands what she is doing far better than we do."[25] Human reason is, perhaps paradoxically, what is responsible for the faulty foundation of what man thinks he knows, Montaigne argues in the "Apologie." Ratiocination is an unhelpful intervention, a filter falsifying cosmic cognition.

Often animal architecture, like the swallows', sparrows', and crows' structures nesting within the pages of the "Apologie," is rec-ognizable even by humans as sophisticated, as possessing a sort of natural technological expertise capable of incorporating such features as ventilation, escape routes, structural stability, and thermoregula-tion. These structures may be constructed by an individual animal, a pair working in cooperation (as in the case of the swallows), or an entire "tribe" of animals acting in concert. And yet, Montaigne notes, as far as we can tell, *no thought* went into these structures. The birds just do it. *We* cannot do that.

Today scientists have come to acknowledge that the process of creating such structures may indeed to some extent involve language; a pedagogy shared among like animals, old to young, experienced to inexperienced; manipulative technologies ,including the use of tools; and even an applied aesthetic sensibility.[26] Montaigne refers to the possible, even likely, existence of linguistic systems among animal species in the "Apologie": both gestural language, which humans themselves possess ("What about hands? We request, promise, call, send away, threaten . . . with [gestures] of a variety and multiplicity that [spoken] language might well envy. . . . There is no movement that does not speak"), and vocalizations ("A certain dog's bark alerts the horse that [he feels] angry; another particular dog's voice does not alarm the horse at all") appear, like a language, to have pattern, intention, and significance.[27] "In sum, we obviously discover that between [animals] there exists full and entire communication and they understand each other, not only within one species, but also across various species. . . . Even among animals without voice, by the kind of arrangements that we can see among them, we can easily make the argument that they have some other form of communication: their movements speak and deal with matters."[28] Only humans appear to lack the discernment necessary to comprehend fully this cross-species communication among animals. In fact, if humans are unable to discern animal language, Montaigne states, this is due to a deficiency in man: "This failing that hinders communication between animals and ourselves, why should it not be attributable to us rather than to them? It's a guessing game who is at fault when we don't understand each other; for we do not understand them any better than they do us. For this very reason, [animals] could consider us stupid beasts [bestes], just as we think they are."[29] Montaigne's assertions predate Father Bougeant's assertions that animals do, indeed, possess language, and he probably influenced Bougeant's thinking. Like Bougeant later, Montaigne argues, although with much less development than Bougeant, the case for animal language, developing his argument, in part, from the ability of deaf-mutes to signify among themselves and to an instructed observer also: "Why [should not animals have speech], just as our deaf-mutes debate, argue, and tell stories by signs? I have seen some deaf-mutes so flexible and clever at doing that, that in truth they lacked nothing to make themselves be perfectly understood."[30]

Abetted by their various types of communication strategies in their "societies," the most prolific builders, other than man, are birds, arachnids, and insects such as bees or wasps; some crustaceans, arthropods, amphibians, and mollusks also build. Their constructions, while probably instinctual, to us nonetheless seem intentional and well suited to specific circumstances and needs. While human buildings are usually constructed to provide shelter, animal structures are also intended to catch prey and to facilitate intraspecies communication. (In contrast with intra-*species* communication, it is worth observing that intra-*confessional* communication was certainly not a goal, and was not possible, in the devastated church structures described earlier—a failure on the part of any religion, where the tolerant Montaigne is concerned. How much easier it is, Montaigne finds, to admire the swallows' structure, with its lack of faith-laden baggage.)

Thus builder birds epitomize for Montaigne *lived strategies of knowing:* they represent and enact a hermeneutics drawn from nature that man, to a lesser degree, may learn to imitate. Montaigne here reverses the customary Christian hierarchy of dominion theology, in which man is deemed "created a little lower than the angels" and all other creatures are subordinate to him. Avian authority trumps biblical authority as the swallows sketch a strategy for knowing. Their scissored tails shape the letter L, evoking the homonym "elle," which may designate the feminine force of Nature in contrast to the male authority ("il") of God. The "elle" also recalls the rebuslike shapes favored by many Renaissance writers such as Tabourot Des Accords and Pelletier du Mans: if we place the swallow in each of the four corners of this page, imitating its search for the best place to build his nest, we find an L angled into each end. This L shape constructs a square recalling the mason's square, to which Montaigne referred in the quotation above ("quarrée"), and thereby comparing the swallows favorably with human master builders, as well as constructing a frame that both protects and contains knowledge. This is the sure space of knowing, Montaigne tells us: the one established and bound by instinct.

One aspect of this knowing is revealed in the swallow's knitting together of its nest. Many birds and insects build with materials that are self-secreted, as in the case of the silkworm or the spider, or collected and then painstakingly and instinctively fashioned into structures themselves. The latter is the strategy of the swallow, which collects feathers from larger birds, soft twigs, horsehair, and other materials and then weaves them into a bowl-like shape. Weaving is *textus;* this textile is, then, a text, a natural construction of a form of knowing. Swallows also form the base of their nests from mud, which they collect and paste to the sides of buildings. This is somewhat rare; only 5 percent of all birds use mud for building, and, in this, swallows may be seen to imitate God, whom the Hebrew Bible describes as taking mud or soil and, from it, shaping man (Hansell 1984, 35). Perhaps this is an early clue that the swallow functions not just on the literal level but also in the figurative and symbolic senses in the "Apologie"; the route of its flight and the sense of its structures ultimately designate a metaphysical referent for Montaigne.

By evoking the swallow's building, Montaigne is directly diminishing the authority of the Renaissance process of *imitatio* and *innutritio:* one learns and then composes a compilation from other authorities, just as he does in his *Essais.* In summarizing the work of Raimond Sebond, Montaigne enumerates various techniques and methods for arriving at certainty—those of the Stoics, Epicureans, Catholics, Protestants, and others. The analogous activity for Montaigne with the builder birds is his citational strategy. He builds a web or nest of authorities nestled within the larger space of his textual presentation, weaving in Pliny, Lucretius, Seneca, Dante, and other authorities much as a bird interlaces found objects deemed suitable to aid in constructing a nest. But reason intervenes in his project, whereas the swallows act faultlessly and from instinct. Human intellectual endeavors, characterized by Montaigne as *ramasser* and *rapiecer,* heaping up and cobbling together, are contrasted with the directed, inherent structuring work of the swallow, the act of *fureter,* or seeking out an appropriate context for knowing and experiencing.

In some respects, Montaigne is practicing the strategy that he uses in the more personal *essais,* especially those of book 3: his composition, while in part based on others' materials, becomes uniquely his own, an individual and embodied structure of what he knows, a personal composite, a construction eventually and ultimately derived from experience and self-assaying rather than from reliance solely on intellectual assent to authorities. In just this way the swallow uses found material that the bird then puts to new use and transforms into his nest, his own product, woven with pieces found elsewhere: a *bricolage.* Montaigne commends this sort of structure and this sort of experiential knowledge.

Since there exists no ultimate noetic certainty, Montaigne maintains, what matters is that we create sense for ourselves, a significance that derives from our life experience and needs and is salubriously limited to our particular circumstances or perspectives. As he reiterates elsewhere, notably in "De l'expérience": "I would rather understand things for myself than [through] Cicero. From the experience I have of myself, I find that I possess sufficient wisdom."[31] The swallow's nest is emblematic of such structure, but Montaigne reproduces the sound of another bird, the dove or pigeon, when describing this utter impossibility of knowing anything permanently or for certain, except for what arises in our own context and circumstances: "Finally, there is no certain and sure existence, neither of our being nor of that of objects. And we, and our judgment, and every mortal thing, goes along flowing and rolling [*coulant et roulant*] ceaselessly."[32] *Coulant* means flowing, and *roulant* means rolling along. But the two taken together are onomatopoetic of the dove's cooing (*roucoulant*): nature is process, nothing stays the same, and our knowledge, claims Montaigne, is most clear and true if it, too, evokes the instinctual constructions of birds and animals. He is perhaps most like a spiritist in this statement, in that the dove also calls to mind the Holy Spirit, and the third person of the Trinity, which is said to "blow where it listeth," to be more airborne, not tied to earth or constrained by convention, not likely to pass judgment or to settle for one creed, a fitting emblem for Montaigne's own tendency toward religious toleration: "Consequently nothing can be proven for certain on either side, and the judger and the judged are in constant motion and exchange."[33]

Montaigne figures himself as a swallow, for, like that bird, he returns again and again to the structure he has built, adding to it. Indeed, Montaigne's famed *allongeails* resulted in at least three complex variations on the *Essais* during his lifetime; like the swallow, he returns from migration to his text/nest, continuing his experience within it, adding to and modifying it. Though the swallow travels far (perhaps not coincidentally, Montaigne set off on his partial grand tour of Europe that resulted in his *Journal de voyage* shortly after completing this essay), it always returns to the same place, and its measuring capacities are always accurate, unlike the mason's square—or other manmade technological tools—that are skewed and out-of-true.[34] Montaigne nests within his text, and the swallow is a new *devise* for him, as it texts—weaves a hermeneutic construction—within the space of this nest. It is instinctual indwelling, rather than reason—the artificial "structures of our wisdom," "reason . . . [made of] lead, of wax, stretchable, bendable, accommodating every inclination"—that Montaigne illustrates and recommends in the "Apologie," through the medium of the swallow.[35]

The attempt to know anything at all is a constant quest, Montaigne tells us. This search, this *queste*, is itself a phenomenon of nature and instinct, not intellect: "Nature abandons us to chance and luck, to search, by art, for those things necessary to our preservation; and she consistently refuses us to give us the means to aspire, by any endeavor or intellectual effort, to the level of animals' natural ability: in such a way that their brutish 'stupidity' surpasses in every way anything that our 'divine' intelligence can pretend to."[36] The term *queste*, associated with the verb "to build" and the *arondelle,* or "builder bird," is repeated throughout the "Apologie," constructing a network of significance around the swallow and its constructive activity. The swallow is also associated with Hermes, the swift messenger god and also the god of knowing; in Ovid's *Metamorphoses*, from which Montaigne frequently quotes, Mercury is often accompanied by birds such as the dove, the hawk, and the goose.[37] Indeed, Mercury, the birdlike winged god, forms part of Montaigne's *devise,* the equilibrated scales with the phrase *Que sçay-je?*, for Mercury's Christian counterpart is St. Michael, whose name Michel de Montaigne shares. In stating, "My scales are uneven and unreliable" and asking, "What assurance do I have that I am right this time, as opposed to others?" Montaigne expresses the same refusal to judge that he exhibits in his cultural relativism. His suspension of judgment is paralleled in his text by the swallow's suspension of her nest, the product of her experiential and instinctual knowing, from the four corners of the *Essais* and from the rafters of humanity's wrecked ideological structures, be they Catholic or Protestant.

Similarly, even that which we believe we know must remain in a state of suspension, its certainty deferred until it can be tested in our daily lives and circumstances, although man's quest does stabilize when man crafts for himself after the pattern of the swallow: his own internal architecture, structured on natural components and his own contextual ("contexture") experience. Then *branle* (incessant shaking, change, and mutability) will cease, if only for a while, as the activity of building brings shape and solidity to man's individual intellectual enterprise.[38] In this way, in one of the most developed and significant essays of his entire oeuvre, Montaigne embeds the solution to the puzzle of comprehension.

The theological affiliation between man and swallow remains the most significant tool through which Montaigne has developed the argument of the "Apologie," and elsewhere in the *Essais* he returns to his theme of how much man can learn from animal, especially when he recognizes the value of the animal kingdom as part of creation along with man: "Let no one mock at this understanding I have with [animals]; even theology orders us to have some care for them and, since the same Master has lodged us all together in this palace for his service, and since they are, like us, members of his family, theology rightly enjoins us to have respect and affection for [animals]."[39]

Animals and Metaphor: Contemporary Comparisons

Several contemporaries of Montaigne also used animal imagery to talk about issues of authority and authorship, though generally in a less philosophical or theological, and more secular, vein. For Pierre de Ronsard, born in 1524 in the rural Vendômois, animals were linked with his personal and experiential love of the countryside; he spoke often of it and visited it frequently. In "Les Louanges de Vandomois," he wrote,

> In short, no matter where I roam
> As long as Heaven will be kind to me,
> This little corner of earth, my home,
> Sweeter than any other will be.[40]

Ronsard spent his first eleven years in a manor house in the country. It may be because of the nostalgic memories of this Eden-like experience that he often styled himself "Pierre de Ronsard, Gentil-homme Vandomois," on his frontispieces. In his elegies, Ronsard reacted vehemently against the logging of big sections of lands his family had formerly superintended. He mourned the loss of habitat for the stag and hinds and even spoke of the discomfiture of the homely sheepdog in "Contre les bucherons de la forest de Gastine."

At the age of fifteen he was sent to the Ecurie royalle, the royal stables, at Tournelles (today's Place des Vosges) in Paris. This was an equestrian academy that taught boys to ride and to wage war and prepared them to become pages. From this experience, Ronsard retained many memories of horses and equine activities that later embellished his poetry. In his *Odes* of 1550, he reworked the myth of Bellerophon, who attempted to tame the legendary winged horse Pegasus. The trick to the taming was a magical bit given to Bellerophon by Pallas Athena when she appeared to him in a dream. In this way, the horse's magical power and physical prowess could be maneuvered and directed by the human who rode him. Ronsard's reworking of the Bellerophon story recalls Montaigne's prescription for effective learning and his use of the metaphor of horse and rider for the pedagogic process. The detailed quality and accuracy of the animal imagery in this and other poems demonstrate Ronsard's experience with, and affinity to, horses, as well as other creatures.

Ronsard's use of mythology to express his feelings about nature and animals is also typical of his approach to poetic composition. While nature is everywhere present in his poems, it is virtually impossible, in many places, to separate reference to nature from mythological allusion: "For Ronsard, nature and mythology belonged to the same universe."[41] So Ronsard both develops and best understands his own textual creations through these combined influences, in a composite making similar to Montaigne's method.

At the age of twenty, Ronsard returned to Paris, where he enrolled to study with the famed poet Dorat at the Collège of Coqueret, one of the great colleges of the University of Paris system. Dorat taught his students that a moral truth should undergird any great poem, and Ronsard adopted this viewpoint, first illustrating it in his *Quatre premiers livres des odes* (1550) and in *Le bocage*, a collection of some earlier poems. It is clear from these early endeavors that Ronsard thought of himself as one who portrayed and imitated nature. He believed that nature was a rich, diverse, and abundant treasure trove. In two sorts of odes, the Pindaric (more grand) and the Horatian (more familiar), Ronsard wrote about his experiences in nature.

Nature and its application to humanity, through the moral lessons illustrated by animals, thus intertwine. For instance, Ronsard evoked the bee as a primary referent for his *furor*, or poetic inspiration: it flies, like the Spirit, where it will, and *butine*, or forages, from selected sources, from which fine stuff it manufactures honey, the symbol of consummate versification. Montaigne expressed his process of construction similarly: "Bees pillage flowers here and there, but afterwards they make honey out of the pollen, and this honey is all their own; it is no longer either thyme or marjoram: just so, from pieces taken from another, the poet transforms and combines to make a work entirely his own."[42] Ronsard also wrote frequently about the flea as an emblem of lascivious desire, hopping about energetically to suck on exposed flesh. The flea acts similarly to some of Ronsard's more bawdy verse. Ronsard admired Rémy Belleau (1528–77), humanist, Hellenist scholar, and Pléiade poet, whom he called "Nature's painter" and whom Albert-Marie Schmidt described as a writer who "intends to reflect all of nature in his work."[43] In particular, Belleau's *Petites inventions* (1556/2005), a collection of six animal *blasons*, received Ronsard's praise and prompted his emulation of them.

In 1552, Ronsard began to write about his romantic experiences. The *Premier livre des amours* speaks of sensual desire and his love for Cassandre, daughter of a Florentine banker. Nature takes on cosmic proportions, and animals such as the swan, in the tale of Leda and the swan, are conscripted into Ronsard's poetic universe to describe the metamorphoses he endures in the throes of love. The second book of *Amours*, written for the peasant girl Marie, is even more rustic both in tone and in setting. Here Ronsard cultivates what he terms a "beau stil bas" and evokes humble and quotidian insects and animals such as butterflies and the honeybee (whose thighs are laden with pollen and drip with honey—an evocative and suggestive image for desire).

In his subsequent *Odes, Amours, Livre de folastries,* and *Chansons,* Ronsard often referred to birds and animals. His "Ode à l'alouette" (1554) is a *blason,* a genre often typified by the use of *animalia.* Ronsard's lark imitates human speech ("mille discours"), probably the love-struck poet's voiced pleas ("conte . . . tes amours"), the lyric verse approximating onomatopoeia:

> No sooner have you been sprinkled
> At break of dawn, with dew,
> You fill the air with wordy sparkle
> And, suspended from the sky, you
> Babble to the winds of your loves.[44]

In addition to the lark, Ronsard writes about swallows, nightingales, turtledoves, and, again, the honeybee.[45] The *Hymnes* (1555, 1556), too, contain numerous mentions of these creatures. Ronsard's "Hymne des astres" situates the stars in relation to "birds, fish, beasts of field and wood," much as does Du Bartas's encyclopedic cosmological tableau *La sepmaine* (see chapter 3).[46]

Even a cursory reading of Ronsard's *Amours* and *Continuation des amours* and a scanning of first lines in which reference is made to animals shows that the poet repeatedly draws connections between animal imagery and the act of authorship. For instance, in the *Continuation* (1555), no. 63, the dolphin features as an intermediary between nature and the gods and possesses special knowledge, which he is able to communicate across species. The final reference of the poem is to the poet himself, who burns with a love so intense that the dolphin fears the oceans will ignite and hastens to warn Cupid of the impending conflagration. So the dolphin acts as a vehicle for the poet to express his own sentiments. The aging warhorse in the *Nouvelles continuations* (1556), no. 1, is given relief from harness and put out to pasture; Ronsard contrasts with this his experience of enduring torment in love but never being given surcease. In the *Amours* (1552–53), no. 117, the nightingale sings all night and harmonizes with the frustrated lover's moans; he is the *porte-parole* of the poet, who identifies the *rossignol*'s song as his own lament: "this bird, who summarizes my complaints."[47] The nightingale recurs in other poems, such as no. 43 in the *Continuation*, where this time he is not the poet's *doppelgänger* but his rival: "Both of us sigh . . . however, Nightingale, there is one difference between us: it is that you are loved, and I am despised."[48] The lady will listen to the bird's vocalizing but plugs her fingers in her ears, refusing to listen to Ronsard's poetizing.

In no. 60, the stag that wanders free in the forest is likened to the lover struck by Cupid's arrow; both lose their freedom through wounding. The image of a biting insect sucking the lady's blood, then being beseeched by Ronsard to bring the blood to him to sip, focuses in *Les amours diverses* in a foreshortened, very detailed way on the insect's anatomy: "double-winged, elephant snout, bloodsucking tube . . . your tiny body, and your mastiff's nose."[49] The insect does the poet's bidding, bringing the blood in an intercessory, almost sacramental way; the animal is a quasi-priestly agent, and Ronsard, through the insect, tells his lady that he has been able to "prendre ton essence": he has supped of her (body and) blood.

During the Wars of Religion, from 1559 until 1563, Ronsard, again like Du Bartas, became a *poète engagé*. Ronsard was a devout Catholic who used his poetry to combat Calvinism. Developing the theme of *homo homini lupus*, he used animal references in a very different way from that of the Protestant poet. Eschewing Calvinist dominion theory, Ronsard invoked a more mystical notion, the prophet Isaiah's "peaceable kingdom," where the lion would lie down with the lamb, as an idyllic reference point to which he hoped France, torn by war, could someday return. Animals would populate this new paradise:

> The stars of heaven, and all the scaly dwellers
> within the sea, the great monsters of the deep
> all that lives in earth, and the airy birds
> which, hanging in the air, float upon the winds,
> all are filled with love, and sustained by it.
>
> (Jones 1970, 177)

Ronsard draws his high notion of the poet-*vates*, the inspired writer, directly from nature as God's mirror. Nature magnifies God's glory, which the poet then takes up and displays, further enhanced, in his verse. Ronsard uses the animal kingdom as a medium for awareness and for deep understanding that extends beyond rational thought to a sense of intuition that imitates the instinctual behavior of animals.

For purposes of comparison and contrast, it is instructive to look at the prose works of a contemporary of Ronsard, Montaigne, and Du Bartas: Noël Du Fail. Du Fail's *Propos rustiques* contains numerous references to animals and varied cultural symbolism associated with different species in order to comment on the vagaries of the human character and condition. His "Banquet rustique," for instance, is an encomium of country life that shows humans and animals interacting, to mutual benefit, in everyday situations. Du Fail enshrines village life as it was before the Wars of Religion and holds it up as a model of what has, tragically, been lost. As Du Fail shows it, animals and men then coexisted in a harmony like that before the biblical Fall:

> After having heard your alarm clock, which is your rooster (a more reliable alarm than those found in towns), you get up gladly, your stomach happy and your head clear (unlike some town drunks!). And yoking your oxen (which are so well trained that they come before you call them), you go to the fields, singing loudly, with no fear of waking anyone else. And there you are entertained by a thousand birds, some singing from hedgerows, others following your plow (showing you great intimacy and affection) to eat the little worms that show up in the turned earth. (Du Fail 1547, 3:16)

This bucolic description antedates the devastation of the religious wars and depicts man and animals at play in the fields of the Lord.

Du Fail believed that some animals and birds were augurs or offered omens, as did Bonaventure Des Périers, another contemporary *conteur* who argued that animals possessed and displayed wisdom. In Des Périers's *nouvelle* no. 87, the mother magpie praises her young for being wise beyond their years: "'Oh!' The mother magpie says, 'do you already know so much!'"[50] As in the tale of the horse (a bit like Balaam's biblical ass) that refused to enter an area known to be haunted until his master said the prayers for the dead, animals have authority: "The priest . . . relied only on his horse's authority to confound the ignorant who denied the reality of purgatory, even though everybody else always had to cite all sorts of textual authorities to prove this point," Des Périers maintains (1561, 564).

For Du Fail as for Montaigne, the wisdom of animals should be heard and heeded more than books or Bible, custom or tradition. Animals signify something that man may interpret to his benefit or ignore to his detriment: "[In the fields the birds] show you signs of the future, and other prognostications, which you have learned through nature and through tradition to understand, such as: The pensive heron, when immobile at water's edge, means winter is not far off; the swallow, skimming the surface of the water, predicts rain; when it flies high in the air, the swallow predicts fair weather; . . . the blue jay going to its nest earlier than usual in the evening shows that winter is approaching; cranes flying high say that the day will be clear and fine . . . ; when geese and ducks keep diving, that means rain is not far off" (Du Fail 1547, 617). Rémy Belleau also speaks of how birds, animals, and even insects, such as "le ver luisant de nuit" (firefly), man's every-day companions, "prophesy to the laborer."[51]

Du Fail, Ronsard, Des Périers, writing in a chaotic and turbu-lent context, use animals nostalgically to evoke a fallen order—not necessarily, as will be the case with Protestant poets like Du Bartas, a theologically encoded order but simply the daily round of predictable events. Animals best represent such an order, through their habits, migrations, and dependable routine of existence. The countryside, now devastated by religious wars, has provided their context. Now wrecked, village life offers no certainties to either man or beast. If, for these contemporary writers, animals epitomize changing social circumstances, for Ronsard they can, as they do for Montaigne in a parallel application, raise changing notions of composition, author-ship, and authority.

Ronsard's status as official court poet complicated and problema-tized his workings-out of matters of authority. His Catholicism con-trasted with Du Bartas's Huguenot perspective, while his position as *chef de file* of the Pléiade, the band of poetic brothers self-appointed to renew French poetry and to invigorate its standing internationally, made him sensitively attentive to animals as figures of invention, imagination, inspiration, and artistic freedom—rather less philosophical than Montaigne's concerns, but not unrelated.

In one of his final poems, the "Dialogue de Ronsard et des muses delogées," the poet, nearing death, is bemused by a flock of cranes flying overhead because, he notes superstitiously, they are flying, not in the customary V formation, but rather in a sinister battle formation. The V—here absent, yet evoked—is like the swallow tail's suggestion of a sketched L: a figured, imaged, animal-metaphoric way to apprehend nature and to comprehend life beyond intellectual cognition. Ronsard's very last poem was literally a swan song, with a *cygne* featuring in the *Derniers vers*.

In every case, the animals so employed are equally valued; their functionality in the text is predicated not on their usefulness alone but on their capacity to surpass textual description or natural historical analysis. Paradoxically, the animals, once construed to be the "lower order," recall Renaissance man to his better self, ranked "one step lower than the angels." Animals thus feature as true mediums— links between heaven and earth, between knowing and not-knowing, in an equation where animals are primary referents and man the mere recipient of the knowledge they have to offer. Balaam's ass—so much more prescient and "seeing" than his obdurate master the purported "seer" and prophet—is a fine emblem for how early modern France respected animal life.

Beyond Montaigne: Seventeenth-Century Applications for Animals

St. François de Sales and other seventeenth-century writers like le père Bougeant were to recall the ultimate metaphysical orientation of Montaigne's essay on Raimond Sebond, despite its lack of religious *parti pris*. He is their great precursor in that, in the final sentence of the essay, sending Mercury winging through the skies and commending the swooping swallow's structures of significance above any human construction, Montaigne designates the heavens as that toward which nature tends. God is the sole certain noetic construct. Montaigne uses an architectural metaphor to contrast humanity's fruitless quest after certainty and deference to established authority with the stable knowing that resides in God: "O God! What do we not owe our Creator for having unburdened us of our naive and deceived notions, and for having *lodged* [our faith] *on the eternal foundation* of His Holy Word!"[52]

The essay becomes a map, or an architectural blueprint, for a new metaphysics knitting together heaven and earth. The swallow's weaving together of knowledge shapes a fabric consubstantial with Montaigne's project in the "Apologie," which he refers to as the *noeud,* or "knot," of the essay, as it tries to ball together and wind up the various yarns of knowledge and experience into the textile of the text: "the knot that should tie up our judgment . . . that should link our soul to our Creator . . . must be a knot whose twists and turns . . . are formed not by our considerations, or by our reasons . . . but by divine bindings."[53]

Where the swallow's structure is concerned, such a knot is unitary: it concentrates what is known into a compact space, as the nest hangs architecturally plumb. Montaigne's meaning hangs suspended from the corners of his text, swallow's nest-like, in those angles that set boundaries where one may always return to what is known and knowable. And what he can know is, must be, tested by personal experience rather than deriving from pure intellect, which deceives; he must emulate the animals and their construction through intuition and instinct: "Isn't it better to suspend judgment than to wander in all the errors that human fantasy has produced? Isn't it better to suspend one's opinion than to take part in seditious discord?"[54]

A "suspension de jugement" figuratively recalls the swallows' nest suspended from four firm fixtures, posts in the corner of a barn or outbuilding. What better way to be certain of something than to doubt its intellectual veracity and to test its literal solidity, to allow the text to be guided by the nest, man to be led by *bestes*? Yet, like the swallow who will always fly off and migrate far, Montaigne finds that the farther we wander, the more we return to ourselves—and we know ourselves, instinctually, in our relation to what lies beyond ourselves, what cannot be housed in any structure, but with which swallows and doves and other birds have some contact as they fly through the empyrean, skimming the surface of the heavens.

CHAPTER
TWO

JOB'S HORSE AND OTHER CREATURES

Animal Analogies in Du Bartas's Protestant Poetics

Hast thou given the horse strength?
Hast thou clothed its neck with thunder?
He paweth in the valley and rejoiceth in his strength.
He mocketh at fear, and is not affrighted.
　　　　　　　　　— Job 39:19 – 25

Subdue it. *He [God] confirms what he had said before respecting dominion. Man*
had already been created with this condition, that he should subject the earth to
himself; but now, at length, he is put in possession of his right, when he hears what
has been given to him by the Lord.
　　—John Calvin, *First Commentaries on the Book of Moses Called Genesis*

"I Have You in My Eye"

In the 1980s feature film *The Madness of King George*, a physician
and former man of the cloth is able temporarily to arrest the slow
and frightening descent into madness of England's monarch by reas-
suring him that he holds him firmly in his gaze: "I have you in my
eye, Sir; I have you in my eye." This statement, somewhat menacing-
sounding but nonetheless effective in stabilizing the troubled monarch emotionally and spiritually, however briefly, not only makes good
sense psychologically but also is a faithful rendering of Protestant theology. God is the all-knowing eye, a motif that was taken up in the
Enlightenment in a disembodied ocular image conveying the sense of
God's—and, eventually, of humanity's—reason as all-knowing.

For the Calvinist Guillaume Salluste Du Bartas, the ultimate referent of his encyclopedic poem *La sepmaine* is the human mind, stretching and exulting in the extent of his access to, and ability to acquire, knowledge, as well as his ability to embrace (and, conceivably, to use and abuse) the power that knowledge provides. Yet Du Bartas's conclusion remains conservative: he exalts humanity at the expense of animals. The animals he describes are possessed and palmed like curios, turned over and scrutinized like treasures, relegated to the status of what is known, labeled, and thereby limited. The actor is man; animals passively receive the effect of his dominating gaze. The text does not allow them an autonomous existence (in contrast to the texts of St. François de Sales and le père Bougeant, explored in chapters 3 and 4).

Recently animal rights theorists have turned their attention to the phenomenon of zoo keeping. Once the purview of monarchs, a showcase of exotica and a pleasure palace, later a popular form of amusement, zoos have been described by Ralph Acampora (2008, 502) as tantamount to a form of pornography. In desubjectivizing the animal, rendering it an object, erasing its wildness, its freedom, and its essence, zoos perform a form of abusive ocular domination, what Acampora has deemed "visive violence" (2008, 502), all for the purposes of humanity's titillation or, at the very least, so that humanity may possess, catalogue, and contain all known forms of life. The gaze both glides over and glancingly grazes, placing the animal in visual subordination.

It is striking how often another gaze, that of the eye of God, reappears in Du Bartas's *La sepmaine*. And while I certainly would not want to equate that divine gaze with the gaze of pornography, it is hard not to see the similarity in terms of domination through the eye, a panoramic possessing and a scoping out of all creation held in visual thrall. Du Bartas himself admits that his subject sometimes threatens to escape him in its immensity and diversity. His encyclopedic goal is penal: to contain, to name, to label, and to confine. And his project is, as he himself acknowledges, dauntingly vast in scope: "Others think that I have industriously sought out various digressions and other distractions in order to make a vain show of my ability. But I am putting them on notice that henceforth I am entering into a great sea of stories that I cannot avoid, even if I try to confine my speech and hinder my style, making less than four really large books."[1] The "grande mer," a maternal sea, from which Du Bartas fishes this plethora of stories seems a teeming, amniotic, and superabundant Nature. Again we find a suggestion that Nature is a woman, and women, like beasts, threaten by their unknowability and uncontrollability. The Calvinist God will need firmly and fixedly to bend his gaze to "hold this slippery and multifarious female and animal Nature in [his] eye" (Acampora 2008, 504).

Du Bartas's Calvinism instructs him that God is both the first and the ultimate spectator of what God has created and that he is entertained by his own creation ("he takes pleasure in seeing"),[2] just as a monarch would be diverted by his princely zoological garden: "He laughs with joy in his heart / and keeps his eyes fixed on his work. / Sometimes he glances over at a meadow where a lamb is frolicking."[3] God's primary act throughout *La sepmaine* seems to be one of seeing: "He sees then how the boat-bearing sea / Receives homage from the water of all the rivers. / He sees that, elsewhere, the sky is breathing in the waves";[4] "His eye, which for a time looks at nothing other."[5] And seeing is holding, possessing, controlling ("il tient toujours").

Consequently, Du Bartas finds that it is right and fitting for man, the zenith of the created order, to imitate the Creator by regarding, describing, collecting in his eye, the abundance of creation:

> Just as Eternal God did not create the universe
> For the beasts of the forest, of the sea, of the air,
> But rather for he who could [know], now casting his eye
> Over the salty realm, now over the spread
> Of the earth, . . . then looking up
> At that which, ordered without order, blazes in the heavens.[6]

For Du Bartas, man's gaze—far-flung and dominating ("jettant sa veue . . . sur l'estendue")—fleetingly and transitorily confers significance on a given creature. But significance is granted only *because man is looking at the animal;* it is the object of his gaze ("devers les yeux") and is in no way a subject. The animal serves to illuminate symbolically an awareness of man's superiority; it embodies a catalogue or a summation of attributes but does not possess its own ontological significance.

La sepmaine's theological anthropology and its focus on the creation as God's means of guiding human beings mean that the creature points to the Creator; as Francis Bacon later observed, in a similar vein, "Knowledge . . . concerning God . . . may be obtained by the contemplation of his creatures; which knowledge may be truly divine in respect of the object, and natural in respect of the light" (1605, 34). Although the creatures are enumerated, the reader does not really get to know them in their creatureliness; rather, they are set to a precise and pedagogic purpose. As Du Bartas's contemporary, the Protestant writer Pierre Viret, expresses it: "The Spirit of God shows us in Holy Scripture this whole world displayed there, like a great book of nature, and of true natural theology; and all the creatures feature there, like so many preachers."[7] Du Bartas echoes this sentiment; he conceives of creatures as animated sermons, but the word they display is always subordinate to God's oversight; it is a word drafted by God.

Du Bartas constructs what George Hoffmann calls "a reasoned collection, one possessing significance, indeed a symbolic meaning," yet the incipient "fictionalization of animals" toward which *La sepmaine* occasionally gestures remains, for the most part, in germ, an imagining less important for him than the transcendent certainty of the Creator's dominion.[8] In this, Du Bartas's Protestant perspective can be clearly differentiated from the revisionist Catholicism of St. François de Sales, who, less than a century later, allowed a fuller understanding of the creature and facilitated the beginnings of an interactive imitation between believer and creature in his devotional manual. And le père Bougeant went even further, anticipating an actual sort of conversation between human and nonhuman animal, a noetic narrative construction.

All Creatures Known: The Protestant Encyclopedia

Du Bartas rivaled Ronsard in France for the reputation of preeminent literary figure of his day and received international acclaim for his work entitled *La sepmaine, ou la creation du monde*. The epic poem went into forty-two successive editions between 1578 and 1623, and echoes of it can be found in John Milton, Philip Spenser, Sir Philip Sidney, Jean de La Fontaine, and many other subsequent sixteenth- and seventeenth-century authors. This work at times met also with opprobrium; it was placed on the Papal Index in Spain.

Du Bartas was born in 1544 in Monfort in the Gers and died in 1590. He was one of the most prolific, successful, and highly regarded writers of sixteenth-century France and achieved an international reputation. Born to a family of merchants, Du Bartas studied law in Toulouse, became Sieur Du Bartas upon the death of his father in 1566, achieved his first literary fame with a poem commissioned by the Protestant queen of Navarre, Jeanne d'Albret, and served under Henry de Navarre in the military as well as on diplomatic missions.

La sepmaine, for which he is best known, is a theocentric and anthropocentric work, directly combating Copernican theory. Du Bartas's encyclopedic approach was intended to glorify God by cataloguing divine handiwork. Essentially, Du Bartas proposed as project a poetic reading of the Book of the World, which God had authored, using what Michel Magnien refers to as the "age-old principle" of analogy that was "still flourishing in the seventeenth century."[9]

Stylistically, the *Sepmaine* in many ways intentionally contradicted and critiqued the theories about poetry that Ronsard and the Pléiade had introduced into France. In return, Ronsard reproached Du Bartas, in his preface to the *Franciade*, with having been too literal, too prone to describe reality as it was. He lectured Du Bartas that "the poet should always take it as axiomatic that he should never seek to replicate reality in its entirety in his art, but rather portray verisimilitude and what is possible."[10] However, most critics concur that *La sepmaine* is quintessentially baroque in expression, and the baroque lends itself to hyperbole, deformation, and exaggeration rather than to a prosaic representation of the quotidian. Its irregularities, extravagances, and digressions in some ways remind the reader of Montaigne's wandering thoughts and textual detours. Indeed, the baroque style, studded with the ornamentation and calculated to dazzle, is well suited to the ebullient proliferation of animals in the created order, the celebration of their habits and differences, and the display of an elaborate world fresh from God's hands.[11] "In creation as Du Bartas conceives of it,

[we] can now see creation as a baroque universe, a dazzling image of a labyrinth at the edges of which animals swarm, flowers unfurl, planets vibrate, comets swirl past."[12]

Further, Du Bartas uses metaphor and simile in ways that bear some similarity to Ronsard's recommended uses of these rhetorical figures and others, although Du Bartas's ideological perspective is different and, generally, theological. Du Bartas was one of the most creative Renaissance inventors of neologisms; he fashioned evocative and even onomatopoetic terms with a hyphenated component such as "flo-flottant." Ronsard had called for "the epic poet [to be] a walking encyclopedia of philosophical, medical, botanical, anatomical, and juridical knowledge. Furthermore, [Ronsard] advised the [writer] not to neglect any fact or story pertaining to the nature of trees, flowers, plants, and roots." Ironically, given Ronsard's criticisms of Du Bartas, "[n]one of Ronsard's admirers heeded this advice more thoroughly than . . . did Du Bartas" (Ronsard 1914, 72; Hallowell 1964, 91). Unlike Ronsard, however, who indulged in much polemical writing during the Wars of Religion, Du Bartas did not take a combative or partisan stance. In fact, when critics attacked him, he merely responded that "no matter what, the song of nightingales will make itself heard amid the importunate cawing of crows and the irritating peeping of frogs" and compared his detractors to "spiders and caterpillars," which could produce a "mortel venin" from the very same flowers as those from which bees made honey.[13]

One of the most significant aspects of Du Bartas's treatment of his subject matter is his representation of abundant variety and his repeated use of the trope of *discordia concors*. Each created element, whether fish, insect, or animal, contains within its species such diversity of lifestyle and appearance that difference rather than similarity predominates. Yet "as above, so below": God's order reflects itself in the world he created, just as man is a microcosm of the macrocosm. Despite the proliferation of difference, uniformity and unity ultimately prevail through the imposition of the Calvinist reading grid over the burgeoning variety of creation.

Du Bartas's text was so highly regarded that it was thoroughly glossed by at least two contemporary commentators. Simon Goulart,

Protestant writer and successor to Calvin in Geneva, wrote his commentary four years after the publication of *La sepmaine* (1581, and again in 1585), while Pentaléon Thévenin from the Lorraine, a Catholic, annotated Du Bartas in 1584. Both were inclined to moralize Du Bartas's text in ways that he himself did not. However, Goulart adhered more closely to the text, while Thévenin used Du Bartas in a polemical way; he reread the Protestant in a Catholic sense, seeking to reopen some of the theological dissonance that had led to the Wars of Religion. Scholars have thus been able to study this text through at least two different lenses (a third, an anonymous riposte to Du Bartas, a *Contre-Sepmaine*, also exists) and thereby to understand Du Bartas's audience(s) and readers, as well as his own textual directions to potential readers.[14] Each of the three interpretative pathways is distinct in significant ways. Du Bartas's annotators, continuators, imitators, and critics construct a critical context for this work's reception and influence. The plurality of hermeneutic possibilities renders quite complex a text that would normally be construed simply to adhere to the rubric of Calvinist plain style or *stylus rudus*. Thus, although Du Bartas's encyclopedic compendium in *La sepmaine* presupposes the vantage point of an all-encompassing, omniscient gaze, the multiple textual optics of subsequent glosses complicate such unilinear reading.

Du Bartas's influences and sources for *La sepmaine* are, among others, the Bible and Hebrew scripture in particular; Pliny's explanatory notes on natural history; the biblical commentaries of St. Basil and St. Ambrose, both of whom had written on the creation of the world; and, to a somewhat lesser degree, the writings of Gregory of Nyssa.[15] Du Bartas was somewhat of an "armchair traveler": he usually did not base his descriptions of animals on direct observation. This suggests that what mattered for him in his project was less a personal knowledge about, or contact with, animals than the purpose to which he was setting them and the aim of his book: an encyclopedic venture aimed at englobing and containing, rather than at experiencing or intimately interacting with, the diverse creatures of creation. In fact, he exercises Adamic onomastics: he dominates not only through ocular sweep but also through *naming*. Some of the stylistic extravagances for which critics reproached Du Bartas derive from the same aim. Du Bartas defends his style with the substance from which it derives: he seeks to imitate creation and thereby to contain and control it. In so doing, he himself creates new words and forms: "Since the job of an ingenious writer is to wed pleasure to profit, who will find it odd that I have rendered the description of the countryside in this painting as diverse as nature herself?"[16] Yet these new turns of phrase, just like the animals, fossils, and other creatures he clasps within the covers of his books, all ultimately derive from the Creator's collector's cabinet: "I put in my work no false and counterfeit jewels, . . . but true diamonds, rubies, and emeralds, secreted away in the holy cabinet of scripture . . . and I contribute the little that God has given me to the structure of his holy tabernacle."[17]

The locus of authority for Du Bartas's writing, then, is conservative and traditional. His sources are not dissimilar from customary sources to which Roman Catholic authors referred concerning *animalia*. While this may at first seem surprising for a Protestant, we should not forget that those of the Reformed faith criticized the Roman Catholic Church as a latter-day aberration. John Calvin always insisted that he was reestablishing the pure, uncorrupt form of the Catholic Church in his Calvinist Geneva (MacCulloch 2005, 189). Further, Calvinists claimed that they had reunited with the early Christian Church. They identified with the Israelites in their persecutions; they named their time of trial during the Wars of Religion and subsequent religious persecution the "desert," alluding to the Exodus narrative in the Hebrew Bible; and they felt that they could link back up with the pure form of the church as God had intended it to be. So using as authoritative sources writers such as Augustine, Basil of Caesarea, and others was perfectly legitimate for a Calvinist and was not a surprising choice. But Calvinists differ from Roman Catholic writers in the *way* they reference patristic sources and the uses to which they put them.

Du Bartas's work remains within the parameters of traditional categories. His project is all about what man can know, and therefore *La sepmaine* deals with dominion theology. It is, further, a literary manifestation of the Ramist system for attaining knowledge. Pierre

Ramus (de la Ramée), humanist, mathematician, and convert to Calvinism (ca. 1550), sought to rectify what he considered distortions in Aristotelian schemas of thinking. In what was to become the quintessential Reformed method for treating a body of information, his system proposed diagrams in which branches (*rami*) interlinked with cross-referenced and similar subjects. Ramus (1515–72) remained influential until late in the seventeenth century. An anti-Aristotelian, he wrote many treatises, among them the important *Dialecticae partitiones* (1543), in which he devised a system of summaries, citations, headings, and instances that produced, effectively, a reorganization of information, relying primarily on binary trees as a method for organizing knowledge. Oriented for the most part toward effective biblical exposition, his system was adopted by most Protestant pedagogues and preachers to ensure the logical transmission of knowledge in an orderly way.[18]

Yet Du Bartas goes out on no Ramist revisionary limbs here: while le père Bougeant, a century later, would insist on the existence of animal souls, and St. François de Sales would propose the use of animals as visual stimuli to a new sort of meditation, thereby effecting significant change in the way that animals were viewed and treated in Western thought and writing, Du Bartas remains in the descriptive mode. He uses Ramus's method but does not reorient or reclassify knowledge as a consequence. Ultimately, Du Bartas's work is a catalogue and manifests a totalizing impulse and a collector mentality. Further, though he focuses more on some animals than on others, his attempt to make a comprehensive survey of the animals he discusses prevents him from exploring any aspect of animality in depth and thereby reinforces—or at least certainly does not challenge or revise—authority and the conventional understanding of animal life.[19]

Ultimately, the message of the *Sepmaine* reinforces reason, order, and control. These are construed as God's attributes, with man as God's agent. One would think this emphasis on an orderly world would engender more than a little cognitive dissonance on Du Bartas's part, given that the hostilities and brutalities of the Wars of Religion were still ongoing.[20] But it is possible that Du Bartas's highlighting of man's mastery of nature derives primarily from a different historical influence: the protoscientific (and, sometimes, arguably pseudoscientific) interests of so many French Protestants of the time.

Huguenots are considerably well represented in the ranks of early modern protoscientists interested in early chemistry, dissection, fossil collection, and alchemical experiments. For example, one of the most prominent alchemists of the sixteenth century was Denis Zachaire. Around 1546, Zachaire was summoned to Pau, the court of the king of Navarre, whose consort, Jeanne de Navarre, was a practicing Protestant and father of the future Calvinist Henri de Navarre. Zachaire likely had Protestant sympathies, if he was not an actual convert. Zachaire epitomized how alchemical—and early scientific—research was carried out in early modern France. Like Du Bartas a native of Guyenne in southwestern France, Zachaire was, like Montaigne, educated in Bordeaux, where he became interested in alchemy. He traveled throughout Europe, making contacts with alchemists in Paris, Toulouse, Lausanne, Milan, and Germany, and came to the notice of Henri de Navarre as a result of his extensive contacts and experiments. His method was to scrutinize natural phenomena for the information they could convey, and his approach to knowledge was to read as widely and as deeply as possible in all the authoritative literature: "I bought books on philosophy, ancient as well as modern, part of which were printed while others were written by hand, the *Crowd of the Philosophers*, the good *Trevisan* . . . and other treatises." He also read as much as he could about animals; among these texts he listed *The Complaint of Nature* (Holmyard 1990, 253).

Later, in the early 1600s, Protestant thinkers gathered in *cercles* to perform amateur scientific experiments as well as to discuss theology; one of the reasons for Cardinal Richelieu's decision to form the Académie française was to absorb—and thereby somewhat neutralize—the extent and influence of these Protestant discussion clubs. So the protoscientific impulse, the desire to make sense of the world by enumerating its various aspects, may, at least in part, explain the *Sepmaine*'s textual net widely cast over the animals and creatures of creation. Calvinist theology plays a part, too. Like the faithful and almost transliterated translations of the Psalms that Clément Marot penned, at Calvin's behest, for Reformed worship in Geneva, the pre-scribed method that Du Bartas implements is that of exposition: he does not invent something new but rather adheres closely to what has already been said in scripture. He amplifies or magnifies what he finds there, but he does not contradict or deny its statements.

Animals, therefore, are for Du Bartas the animate and literal-ized form of the workings of God's mind and will. His text is merely the illustration of God's *magnum opus*—a sort of *catalogue raisonné* translating the divinely ordained wonders of nature so that man may comprehend them. Despite his stylistic innovations, and even his occasional apparent deviations from Calvinist exegetical guidelines, Du Bartas, for the most part, epitomizes dominion theology.

From Alpha to Zoophilia

Du Bartas's work teems with animal, bird, and insect life. Among the species he mentions are elephants, rhinoceroses, lions (including the legend of Androcles and the lion), horses, dogs, rams, and stags, as well as the fabled unicorn and dragon; nightingales, the mythical phoenix, peacocks, owls, pelicans, hens and roosters, sparrows and eagles; scorpions; many types of fish and reptiles; and a variety of insects. Of the seven *jours* in *La sepmaine*, days 2 and 5 are especially rich in their depiction and evocation of creaturely existence. Like medieval bestiaries, the *Sepmaine* generally provides an enumeration of varieties of animals, then characterizes most of them with an adjec-tive or a short observation concerning their life-ways. Du Bartas is even more thorough in his enumerative strategy than La Fontaine a century later, who certainly was ambitious in his scope: "The animal is still an instrument, but it also has a real role to play in La Fon-taine's work. There are 104 animal fables, in which over 125 different animals feature. The most popular is the wolf (26 times), then the fox, dog, lion, donkey, rat, cat, sheep, and mouse. . . . In total, 450 appearances of animals on the fabulist's stage."[21] At times, Du Bar-tas expands on his recitation, developing fledgling narratives, and in this he is much different from medieval predecessors. The narrative aspect reads much like the focus on textual development found in sermon exposition as practiced by John Calvin.[22]

The occasions on which Du Bartas drafts such digressions or amplifications are important to examine for what they have to say about his sense of the *contemporary* significance of such animal references, as we shall see shortly. Further, occasionally, Du Bartas allows himself to make protoscientific speculations about the animals, showing a deep involvement in the project of attempting to decipher creation, not just to discern the imprint of the Creator (also a medieval and Roman Catholic preoccupation), but also to ascertain the worth and meaning of creation itself. For instance, during the second *jour*, he describes how myriads of frogs appear on the earth after a heavy rain and conjectures that they have ensued from a sort of spontaneous generation (Du Bartas 1981, 531). In its attempt to apply science to scripture, his approach constitutes a somewhat daring departure from the norm, yet it is nonetheless consistent with the spirit of the age and with the Huguenot involvement in protoscience described above.[23]

Du Bartas's work does at times surpass compendium and enumeration, becoming a sensual delight, an irrepressible jubilation faced with the magnificent variety present in creation. As Ann Blair and Isabelle Pantin have commented, "Du Bartas is first and foremost an edifying apologeticist: he aims at unfolding the book of the world and at showing that it was written by God's hand; but the detailed reading of the wonders of nature produces, just on its own, entertainment beyond compare" (2006, 276).[24]

And while Du Bartas's Calvinist beliefs still provide the essential armature for his text, in some instances, "paradoxically," Du Bartas's "specifically Christian . . . way of thinking [was] less prone to emphasize man's superiority to other species. . . . Animals had been created by God for their own sakes, for the 'Gayety' that . . . [could be] discovered in whales and pond mites [for their own sake] rather than for the use of man; consequently, all were deserving of kindness and respect" (Donald 2007, 38). In this, he verges *beyond* the boundaries of scriptural exegesis prescribed by John Calvin. Calvin wanted all scriptural exegesis and exposition to work always to emphasize God's majesty and sovereignty. According to Calvin, man was meant to be

God's agent and, in so doing, also to point inexorably to God's power. He therefore constantly stressed the "pre-eminence" of man over all other creatures, stating that God "appointed man . . . lord of the world [and] . . . expressly subjects the animals to him" (1847, 98).

Obviously Du Bartas, as he expands both medieval models and contemporary hermeneutics, intends something *other* in his text. The "otherness" of animals provides the vehicle for the "otherness" of Du Bartas's thought. This difference remains more stylistically suggested than thematically developed, however: a sort of onomatopoetic writing style evokes the animal, but normally the textual argument does not expand upon the "animalness."

Du Bartas's evocations of different animals and their interactions with members of their own, and other, species are significant stylistically in having a mimetic component. Frequently, he imitates an animal's characteristic sound in his verse, using the alliterative "s" to connote the sibilance of a serpent; evoking, through a word selection, a typical shape, such as the twists of nautilus's shell or snail's curve (in this instance, "entortillé," spiraled); using evocative sounds, or crafting neologisms, such as "ba-battant," to suggest the sounds of animals, or those made by their environment (here, the waves). Indeed, Du Bartas himself describes his style in animalistic terms; the leaps and cavorting of a goat (cf. Montaigne, "à sauts et à gambades") best characterize his technique.[25]

Aspects of Du Bartas's work demonstrate elements of the grotesque, Montaigne's "jumping, frolicking" mode. The grotesque induces a feeling of uncomfortable bizarreness simultaneous with empathy or pity; it is a construction both manifesting and eliciting hybridity equally in form and in response. The grotesque has been interpreted as a crucial device that societies use anthropologically to understand alterity and alteration. For this reason, the grotesque may be a well-chosen stylistic mode for a Protestant writing during the fraught and changing times of the Wars of Religion and attempting to communicate an altered *mentalité*. Using animals further underscores the novelty of the Calvinist vision and allows potential critiques of human nature arising from those wars to cede to a strong ontological narrative, a providential underpinning.

Reading Backwards

The Calvinist sociologist and theologian Jacques Ellul maintains in *Revelation* that revelation has already occurred and that a Protestant perspective should properly read backwards, since what was meant to be accomplished has already been done, in Christ (1977, 236). Ellul illustrates this argument by referring to the Calvinist poet, polemicist, and friend of Du Bartas, Agrippa d'Aubigné, who, in *Les tragiques*, describes a powerful scene (in the book *Fers*) in which tortured Protestants are consoled in their plight by knowing that God has already worked out his purpose (d'Aubigné 1995). Du Bartas's Protestantism works similarly, and it is actually quite instructive to read *La sepmaine* beginning with the last week. The textual perspective is, indeed, hierarchical, with the apogee of creation, man, being described, as the Bible also would have it, on the sixth day of the week. But to begin with the seventh day, that on which God rested from His labors, in fact provides a global view of what Du Bartas has progressively worked toward in this epic poem and its use of, and effect on, animals.

We read backwards, as Du Bartas, like God, looks back. The referent is the sin or the Fall, and we then read backwards from it to a prescription or a proscriptive curb on further sin. The tone is censorious, often scolding, underscoring the rift between what God had expected and hoped for from his most favored creature, humanity, and man's failure to measure up. Most examples of human conduct are negative. Nonetheless, Du Bartas still pays lip service to scripture's characterization of man as creation's highest achievement.

It is instructive that the first scenario described in the Seventh Day, after God has surveyed his global domain, is that of hunting. First, God luxuriates in his visual, and synesthetic, encompassing of the landscape; then a hunter with his gun is shown taking aim at birds in trees. This is not condemned or even seen as a disruption of the natural order; significantly, it is highlighted as a legitimate act of dominion theology. God loves man above all other creatures, "and because he loves man, he loves all [that man does]."[26]

In "The Killing Game: An Ecofeminist Critique of Hunting," Marti Kheel asserts that hunting is the ultimate, prehistoric experience of domination of the natural world as well as erasure of the hunter's suspect female side:

> Hunting may be seen as a symbolic attempt to assert mastery and control over the natural world. . . . Feminist psychoanalytic theory . . . explain[s] . . . boys must not only disidentify [sic] with the mother figure, but they must deny all that is female within themselves. . . . Having established a second and alienated nature . . . men then face a lifelong urge to return to the original state of oneness that they left behind. . . . The pursuit of the animal expresses the hunter's yearning to repossess his lost female and animal nature. The death of the animal ensures that this oneness with nature is not attained. Violence becomes the only way in which the hunter can experience this sense of oneness while asserting his masculine self-identity. (2008, 460)

In this hierarchical universe, man is God's best-beloved, even his proxy. Du Bartas diminishes animal nature by asserting that man, without the gifts that God has bestowed on him, would be merely "une beste sauvage" (Du Bartas 1981, 308, v. 110).

Justice, rather than love, is God's fundamental characteristic with respect to his creation. Unlike "the loving eye" that some animal rights activists have called for to ameliorate our treatment of animals, what ecofeminists have called an "ethic of care" in context, God's gaze is both a-contextual and sternly assessing (Russell and Bell 1996). He is, above all, "juge," the progenitor and maintainer of immutable law that, as though with etching acid, he sears into humanity: "as in each body, with the etching of his finger / He engraves the holy text of a holy law" (Du Bartas 1981, 311, v. 171).[27] God is also depicted as a medieval suzerain, a monarch, "le Président" (311, v. 167). Du Bartas stresses God's power, his work ethic, how well he has established "all manner of thing"; his knowledge derives from the intake of his gaze, and his power proceeds through it:

> He sees clear as day at midnight.
> The deepest chasms seem crystal pools to him.
> His eye sees [what is thought] before it is ever thought.[28]

His omnipotence here finds its fullest expression in his omniscience and omni-seeing. Du Bartas's characteristically Calvinist concern for order and reason leads him to a proto-Cartesian view of the universe as a machine with its interlocking parts calibrated by God: "this great mechanism, which causes the interlocking pieces of this large body [the earth] to play and function."[29]

While the disruption and untidiness of human affairs, such as Du Bartas himself experienced during the Wars of Religion, may seem to give the lie to this divine superintendence and regency, and while "it is true . . . that human matters / seem ceaselessly to flow in uncertain changeability," nonetheless, against all odds and despite appearances, God provides a privileged providential care for humanity, especially for those who worship him: "But with a care even more careful, he covers with his wings / Adam's seed, and especially the faithful."[30] All that happens is by God's reasoning ("estre fait par raison"), Du Bartas stoutly insists (1981, 313, v. 206). The primary concern is that man somehow be rehabilitated, reminded of his lost glory, so that he may attain heaven. Perhaps not surprisingly, despite the purported focus of what he has just accomplished and now sums up in this last book, a compendium of nature's creatures, Du Bartas shows no concern for the plight of animals during wartime, or for the salvation of what he deems a subordinate and inferior order of creation.

The Seventh Day is the Sabbath in scripture, the observance of a day of rest from labor. In the Hebrew Bible, in the book of Deuteronomy and elsewhere, explicit provision is made for animals to rest on the seventh day, too. Du Bartas overlooks this. Man reads the book of creation on the Sabbath and learns from it and may be saved thereby. Indeed, he reads it backwards, as he is now reading Du Bartas's Seventh Day, as are we, and recalling all that has preceded it. The tableau of the transmission of salvific knowledge is significant, as is its tone. Du Bartas instructs his reader: he acts and sounds like a pedagogue, a *magister,* and he seems to sit in God's seat and looks about him with God's gaze; his book is conflated with the Bible.

Du Bartas's tone is one of a contrived proximity, not the intimacy we will glimpse in St. François de Sales's scene of spiritual direction, a situation typified by tender, gentle relational and interpersonal guidance. Nor is the tone anything like what le père Bougeant's textual scintillations will display before his *salonnard* hosts. This contrast is instructive, and quintessentially Calvinist. "Sied-toy donc, lecteur, sied-toy," Du Bartas peremptorily commands his reader, asserting his authority by repeating the order:

> Sit yourself down, reader, sit next to me,
> Talk about these conversations, see what I see,
> Listen to this mute doctor [the world], study in its book,
> Which night and day, being open, will teach you how to
>   live well.[31]

The planetary bodies, the sea and earth and sky, as well as the bodies of animals ("tant de corps"), pose as pedagogues in this great endeavor to learn life aright: "so that so many bodies might be as many good teachers / to create great doctors of those who have no book learning."[32] It appears that nature's primary purpose is to serve as a tool in man's rehabilitation. Salvation is proffered exclusively to the species of mankind.

Teaching Animals

Animals are first students; they study the glory of their Creator in this Protestant portrayal of nature redeemed and man redeemable:

> I see that the elephant,
> Studious scholar, is ruminating on his own
> The lesson taught him: he venerates his king.[33]

In fact, once the elephant has conned his texts, he himself may become a writer. For example, the elephant uses his long trunk to trace his understandings: "Indeed, if Greek [natural] history doesn't deceive us, / [the elephant] sometimes writes with his trunk."[34] And horses are portrayed as already schooled in the *manège* of dressage:

> The horn-hooved horse, quick, ambitious,
> Loves his master, loves war . . .

[Learns], with [no further need of] trainer and without bit
    [in his mouth],
To pick up his hooves, to make turns and circles,
And will follow, without being tied.[35]

Without bridle, bits, reins, or even rider, this horse knows how to execute the finest dressage movements. This is pre-Edenic; the Protestant description shows that postlapsarian nature is what necessitates the pedagogy, a relearning on the part of man, a re-formation of his heart:

Forgive, good Lord; forgive me, it is not you, Lord,
Who troubles the beginnings of happiness in our lives,
It's our pride [that does that] . . .
Before Adam rebelled against you . . .
He lived as king of paradise . . .
The proudest wild animals willingly bowed to him,
Bending their neck beneath his yoke and obeying him
    promptly.[36]

Subsequently, man's fall has necessitated a change in status of animals, insects, crustaceans, and cetapods: all must now function as pedagogues in the Protestant project.

Animals' role is to offer wisdom to man. Their entities, lives, habits, and peculiarities are all described in detail, not because they matter *in se*, but because from them can be gleaned useful knowledge of which man may avail himself. Man goes to school in nature: "So up, kings! Up, vassals! Up, run to the school of . . . / The swarming honey-giving hive . . . of the squirrel . . . of the warm sparrow!"[37] Following the patriarchal Protestant model, Du Bartas instructs the *pater familias* to send his children to study among animals, just as the eagle flies among its young to teach them how to fly:

Fathers, if you want your well-behaved children
To enrich your old age with their own well-being
Put them on the path of unfeigned virtue,

With good teaching, good examples, and fear.
Just so the eagle flutters around his young
To teach them to fly.[38]

The mise-en-scène is didactic and pedagogic. Du Bartas is moralizing, and he is using animals for practical human needs and profit.

These are instructive stories, exempla. A series of righteous animal anecdotes follows: the adulterous woman is instructed to imitate "la tortue," who laments her lost mate all the rest of her life; gossips and wags are negatively contrasted with geese, who know to be silent and cease their honking when near the nests of eagles who might try to seize them; neglectful mothers fare poorly when compared to fish, who have a care for every need of their young; the uncharitable and grasping have much to learn from the dolphin, "who puts himself in the way of harm to his companions" and who demonstrates altruism; and ungrateful children are put to shame by the "chevreuil," who brings food to older goats stranded on the heights (Du Bartas 1981, 330–31, vv. 584–97, 610–12).[39]

It would appear there is no need for books or other instruction beyond that which animals can provide. Even the tiniest insect or spider possess sagacity in abundance: "a single spider has something to teach each one of us."[40] This is the panorama of a wise world. Yet the wisdom is seen as valuable in the way that ore to be extracted from the earth has incipient worth: animal mindfulness is to be mined and measured, doled out as befits specific individual human needs.[41] For instance, kings can learn from the lion "imitating [the lion's] virtue / Which would never attack a fallen soldier," while slatterns and spendthrifts may profit from the example of the "hérisson," which prepares for winter ahead of time.[42] Animal species are treated like simples, or pharmaceutical healing herbs. A particular animal is prescribed for every human moral failing. So subordinated are animals' natures to man's needs that God even makes certain species of animals fight among themselves for man's benefit:

Thus for love of him you have made harmful
serpents toward other serpents . . .

You make it so, O Almighty Lord, that the ungrateful viper
While being born, tears at the entrails of his dying mother."[43]

The Protestant picture of a dominated nature has never been more
thoroughly delineated.

A Calvinist Conclusion

Du Bartas's text is above all significant in that it illustrates how the
late sixteenth century viewed animals. In particular, it exemplifies the
collector mentality that was prevalent, especially among Calvinists
(Schnapper 1998). A consequence of this collector mentality is that
the creature serves to point to the Creator, and Du Bartas is content
with this tendentious treatment; he does not go into great detail concerning the creature's particular characteristics. As Yvonne Bellenger
notes, "This particular poetic sensibility manifests the customary
sentiment concerning nature in the seventeenth century. One loves
nature, but nature as she is not, in truth. One has to confer order
on her, master her. Raw nature doesn't usually fascinate; and one
is very skilled in separating out those animals that are part of one's
idealized nature and those that one does not want to welcome into
that dream."[44] The animal functions more as what has been called
"a living and domesticated tool [used] to fulfill man's needs" and to
designate a metaphysical orientation.[45] This is a quintessentially Protestant perspective, a kind of patriarchal ordering and *prise de contrôle*,
in which nature derives from and illustrates grace but is not built up
on or by grace.

In some respects, Du Bartas's Protestant attitude is, perhaps not
surprisingly given his nonpolemical nature and the encyclopedic aim
of his project, consistent with official Roman Catholic doctrine during
the early modern period, which de Sales most likely unintentionally
circumvents and which Bougeant probably intentionally contravenes.
As Robert Delort notes, this doctrine is "motivated by the need to
mark a difference between animal and human destiny, to affirm the
immortality of the [human] soul" and to affirm the animal's lesser

and lower state so as to avoid the "theological discomfort concerning the status of humanity" that might result from placing a higher valuation on animals' abilities.[46] Thus the animal's authority is never ultimate; it is always only proximate and accessory to humanity's gradual attainment of authority.

In fact, the reference to early modern protoscientific Protestant thinkers, among whom Du Bartas should be included, underscores a salient difference between Du Bartas and Montaigne, his predecessor, in that while for Montaigne the animal has its own status as a sentient being with a mind and the capacity for language, for Du Bartas the animal in general remains at the purely symbolic stage—and that is much more in the pre-Cartesian domain, the authoritative assertion of human rationality as dominant over animal existence.

The Catholic perspective of St. François de Sales, to which we turn next, is very different. De Sales illustrates the Thomist dictum—while in many ways significantly differing from Thomist anthropology—that grace builds on nature. For de Sales, the creature helps man to reach up toward the Creator.

THE FAUNA OF FAITH

Animating Spirituality

*And not only did God communicate to them their being and their natural graces
when he beheld them . . . but also in this image of His Son alone He left them
clothed with beauty, communicating to them supernatural being. . . . He exalted
man in the beauty of God, and consequently exalted the creatures in him, since
in uniting himself with man He united Himself with the nature of them all. . . .
Not only did the Father beautify the creatures [through the Incarnation]. . . . He
left them all clothed with beauty and dignity.*

—St. John of the Cross, *Spiritual Canticle* 5.4

*A Fly has feeling as well as an Ox; and a Toad has as much right of happiness as
a Canary Bird; for the same GOD made the Ox, and the Fly and the Toad and
the Bird. . . . For cruelty to a Brute is odious and abominable, whether it be to a
beast, a bird, or a Fish, or a Worm.*

—Humphrey Primatt, *A Dissertation on the Duty of Mercy and the Sin of
Cruelty to Brute Animals*

Those who are close to nature are the most spiritual souls.

—Meister Eckhart, sermon 1

Why are we by all creatures waited on?

. . . .

*Why brook'st thou, ignorant horse, subjection?
Why does thou, bull and boar, so sillily
Dissemble weakness, and by one man's stroke die,
Whose whole kind you might swallow and feed upon?
Weaker I am, woe's me, and worse than you.
You have not sinned.*

—John Donne, Holy Sonnet XII

The medieval Dominican preacher Meister Eckhart said that if he were to contemplate the tiniest creature, perhaps an insect, sufficiently, he would never need to write another sermon, for that natural creature would summarize and display the Word of God more fully than any sermon (1986, 234). Eckhart's statement was proleptic and prophetic: this medieval theologian, brought up on heresy charges by the contemporary Roman Catholic Church, actually in some ways anticipated the seismic shift in theological perception that was to characterize seventeenth-century Jesuit thinking on animals and authority.

Much of this shift can be framed in terms of theatricality, especially, but not only, in the case of St. François de Sales, whose work is examined below. St. Ignatius Loyola's *Spiritual Exercises* (composed 1522–24) had relied on the concept of stage setting, the theatrical agencing of a spectacle so that the believer could be drawn in through a synesthetic, and often primarily visual, experience to a holistic apprehension of God (MacCulloch 2005, 642). And contemporary Jesuits were particularly known for making an appeal to all the senses, through ballet, opera, and street theater and processions with monstrances prominently displayed (Rock 1996).

St. François was the first to write a manual for the believer that deliberately animated faith through reference to animals, however. In this way he created a new kind of naturalistic authority of experience that surpassed the church's insistence on scripture and tradition as the primary ways of experiencing God. He also demonstrated a trust in and a reverence for the created order that Du Bartas, for instance, did not evince and that may have set the stage for the full-blown theories of le père Bougeant, less than a century later, concerning the existence of animal souls.

A New Sort of Spirituality: The Genre of the Devotional Manual

Catholic theology perceived God's handprint in and on the world. Reading the world as God's Book of Nature, Roman Catholic theologians enumerated the ways, for instance, in which "simples," or herbal medicines, were deemed to bear God's signature: a medieval cloister garden would contain a *pharmakopeia* in which every existing malady would find its antidote through divine provision. This notion derives from the Aristotelian emphasis on *telos*, according to which every plant—or animal, or other being—has specific, knowable traits and a set, defined purpose. Building on this hierarchy, St. Thomas Aquinas instructed, "As all the perfections of Creatures descend in order from God, who is the height of perfection, man should begin from the lowest creatures and ascend by degrees, and so advance to the knowledge of God" (*Summa contra Gentiles*, I, 4, cap. 1; Aquinas 1905).

In many ways, Aristotelian categories influenced both Roman Catholic and Reformed theological understanding of animal life for centuries. Aquinas developed Aristotle's presupposition that rationalism and reliance on logic were fundamental to intellectual inquiry. Thus Aristotelianism undergirds both Roman Catholic and Reformed approaches to revelation and to scripture. This tendency began to emerge in the thirteenth century and became the dominant characteristic of Western thought. Aided by the founding of the Society of Jesus in 1540, scholasticism became the dominant intellectual framework of Catholic Reformation Europe, exemplified by the theology of Robert Bellarmine, Francisco Suarez, and Gabriel Vásquez. But Reformed Protestants also continued to teach Aristotle in their academies: Théodore de Bèze in Geneva and Conrad Gesner in Zurich taught deductive logic and a reliance on reason, a form of Aristotelian revival that has been called a "Second Scholasticism" (Williams 1996, 24).

However, largely because of confessional differences and polemical confrontations during and after the Protestant and Catholic Reformations, these views inevitably diverged. The Protestant view, developed by Guillaume Salluste Du Bartas, had considerable influence throughout Europe. Du Bartas's encyclopedic, descriptive, and representational ordering of reality still seems quite close to that of Aristotle, and, indeed, Du Bartas's influences and sources remain, in part, classical and antique. Du Bartas pens an epic poem designed to stress God's power through a cataloguing of creation and creatures, but these creatures are not set to any purpose in the reader's spiritual life.

A different medium in which notions of animal life began to be set to spiritual service in the late sixteenth and early seventeenth centuries was the genre of the devotional manual. Devotional literature, of course, had existed long before this time. There was a long tradition of devotional manuals in Roman Catholicism, the most venerable ancestor probably being Thomas à Kempis's *Imitatio Christi* (ca. 1450). A brief look at the character of devotional literature prior to the sixteenth century will clarify the specific changes that occurred later.

In general, devotional literature had four components: reading, prayer, meditation, and contemplation. These activities mutually informed each other but were also often structured along a hierarchy, or "ladder," in which the believer gradually came to disassociate himself from the world of the senses in order to attain union with God. The activity of the intellect, gradually dispossessing itself through elevation to God, was preeminent. "Reading is a directing of the mind to a careful looking at the scriptures. Meditation is a studious activity of the mind, probing the knowledge of some hidden truth under the guidance of our own reason. Prayer is a devout turning . . . to God to get ills removed or to obtain good things. Contemplation is a certain elevation above itself of the mind which is suspended in God" (Tugwell 1985, 96). The *Scala claustralium* (or *Spiritual Ladder*) by Guigo II in the twelfth century may be the first formalization of this devotional process known as the *exercitium spiritualis*. Guigo II taught the cultivation of the inner disposition; one was not to be interrupted by distractions of outer existence. The contemplative effect makes one "forget earthly things" (Tugwell 1985, 97).

There was, however, some, though not much, indication in a few contemplative manuals that creatures might be useful or in some way involved in meditation. Hugh of St. Victor, for instance, described in *De meditatione* a three-tiered hierarchy of meditational subjects: creatures, the Bible, and morals (Hugh of St. Victor 1886, 113).

Context and circumstances changed, especially because of the strife of confessional conflict during the early modern era. Shifts in devotional literature probably derive, at least in part, from the post-Tridentine and baroque turn to the sensory world—indeed, recommendation of recourse to elements of it—to create effective and persuasive preaching (Soergel 1993). Meditational manuals became much more oriented toward using the imagination and feeling emotions; Margery Kempe is an example of a meditational strategy that embroidered so extensively on biblical story, in order to insert herself into the text, that she was "not only imaginatively present, but actually a participant" in the event (Tugwell 1985, 109). Occasionally animals populated these daily-life imagined scenarios, primarily as furnishings and props.

After the avoidance of much of the external world, creatures included, manifested in earlier devotional literature, it might be expected that Catholic early modern authors of devotional literature would demonstrate a shift toward the sensory realm, but this was not generally the case. Prior to the Jesuits, it seems that the "ladder" paradigm and the self- and world-denying aspect of contemplation were preeminent. For example, John of the Cross, Catholic mystic and contemporary of St. Ignatius, denied the world and its creatures any role or value in transformative ascesis. And while William of Thierry, author of manuals on meditational prayer, used the phrase "animal prayer," he meant it pejoratively: as a kind of "petitionary prayer, proper to those with no understanding of spiritual things" (Tugwell 1985, 109).

In his meditational work *The Ascent of Mount Carmel*, St. John of the Cross states that "no creature, none of its actions and abilities, can reach or express God's nature. Consequently, a soul must strip itself of all creatures and of its actions and abilities (of its understanding, taste, and feeling)" (John of the Cross 1987, 89). He recommends the "night of the senses," the virtual annihilation of man's sensual attachment to the world, because "of the distance that lies between what creatures are in themselves and what God is in Himself. . . . Souls attached to any of these creatures are just as distant from God" (69).

John of the Cross explicitly opposes the very strategy that de Sales was to put in practice in the *Introduction à la vie dévote*: an intentional attachment of the spiritual seeker to a creature that, through some new kind of relationship, some quintessential activity, has something to teach or to offer the seeker. John of the Cross refuses to encourage such interaction, holding to a strictly delimited, traditional hierarchy of creatures and averring that "all creatures are nothing, and a person's attachments to them are less than nothing since these attachments are an impediment to and deprive the soul of transformation in God" (John of the Cross 1987, 66). So even John of the Cross, often construed as an extravagant mystic, does not deviate from the already established format of devotional literature of the day and age.

And if, for purposes of comparison, we look briefly at the Anglican preacher and poet John Donne, whose work, as a sort of theological hybrid, might manifest aspects of both Protestant and Catholic emphases in devotional literature, we find that he, too, makes little use of the animal kingdom. His focus is more on man, man as microcosm and as a failed and blasted exemplar of God's glory. Everything in the world of the senses—illness, depression, sin, inadequacy, melancholia—serves to remind him of how far man is from attaining union with God.

Donne seems set on underscoring the absolute distance that separates man from God, not in bridging it through creaturely companionship, as does de Sales. In *Devotions upon Emergent Occasions* (1624), Donne insists that "Ants, and Bees, and Flowers, and Kings . . . are all as nothing, altogether nothing, less than nothing, infinitely less than nothing, [compared] to . . . the knowledge of the glory of the Lord" (2001, 492). If there is any hope for the progressive divinization of man, this must happen in the traditional way, contemplatively. Certainly other creatures are not to be consulted or involved: "We attribute but one priviledge [*sic*] and advantage to Man's body, above other moving creatures, that he is not as others, groveling, but of an erect, of a form . . . and disposed to the contemplation of Heaven. . . . Other creatures look to the earth; . . . but Man is not to stay there, as other creatures are; Man . . . is carried to the contemplation of that place . . . his home, Heaven" (2001, 424–45). There is certainly no discussion of an animal soul ("They see the soule is nothing . . . in other Creatures . . . but if my soule were no more than the soul of a beast, I could not thinke so; that soule that can reflect upon itself, consider it selfe, is more than so"); the possession of a soul is assigned only to man and is attested—and Aquinas would have concurred—by man's rational faculty; salvation is foreseen only for the human (2001, 447).

Donne shows some similarity to Montaigne in valuing the experiential and instinctual knowledge of animals, conceding that animals possess ways of treating their ills through natural medicine, while man is utterly dependent on the inadequate knowledge of physicians ("Here we . . . sink in our dignitie, in respect of verie meane creatures, who are *Phisicians* to themselves. . . . The *Hart* that is pursued and wounded . . . knows an Herbe. . . . The *dog* . . . subject to sicknes . . . knows his grasse that recovers him. . . . Man hath not that innate instinct . . . as those inferiour creatures have"; 2001, 426–27). But this recognition of animal wisdom is not sufficient to convince him to provide creatures a place in any soteric schema. In fact, Donne is more likely to portray animals as threats to humanity than to discern positive or helpful attributes in any potential creature-human relationship: "Creatures naturally disposed to the ruine of Man . . . the Flea, the Viper . . . d[o] all the harm [they] can" (2001, 439).

Donne's attitude seems more akin to the "dominion theology" of the Calvinist Du Bartas. He, too, remains within a more conservative understanding of theological anthropology as it is displayed in devotional literature. Donne's *Devotions upon Emergent Occasions* seems, ultimately, more a concentrated self-scrutiny than a method for spiritual progress. The focus remains very androcentric.

It is undeniable, however, that the genre of Catholic devotional literature began to alter significantly during the late sixteenth century and throughout the seventeenth, becoming more manual-like in format and allowing for considerably more (although still carefully patterned) reliance on the working of the imagination in the world of the senses—particularly regarding creaturely existence. Further, the rise of the devotional manual seems to run parallel to the growing interest in natural science; indeed, some theologians applied the term *contemplatives* to natural scientists.[1] The changes in focus and format can be largely attributed to Jesuits—and, influenced by them, Salesians.

Roman Catholic devotional manuals tended to be more mystical in emphasis and tone than other, authoritative, church-sponsored or doctrinal texts.[2] A devotional manual served the needs of individual believers, usually construed as neophytes or "children," and, later, as women, who wanted to advance along the path of belief. It was

therefore designed for the exercise of inner piety rather than an external or ecclesiastic practice of faith. The golden age of the devotional
manual was the seventeenth century, and this is perhaps because
these tracts were often treated somewhat dismissively by ecclesiastical authorities and censors as second-order theology: they were
generally aimed at the laity and could seem somewhat simplistic or
popularizing in tone. Further, even at the beginning they were written exclusively in the vernacular, not the idiom in which matters of
theological import were explicated.

The devotional manual seems to have been, at least in part,
a Catholic Reformation response to some criticisms leveled by the
Protestant Reformation against clerical corruption or tepidness. St.
Ignatius Loyola, a contemporary of John Calvin, in part viewed his
Spiritual Exercises as the forming-ground of a spiritually militant,
young male defender of the Catholic faith, and, indeed, his *Spiritual
Exercises* was one of the most influential early modern prototypes of
the devotional manual in the sixteenth century (Loyola 1991).[3] Unlike
de Sales's devotional manual, St. Ignatius's book is directed, at least
initially, primarily at clergy and those ordained, although the *Exercises*
have a long and important tradition of having been "made" by the laity
as well. First and foremost, this is a text that describes the very particular inner workings of St. Ignatius's own piety, a highly imaged and
vividly imagined structured format leading the believer to reenvision
key scenes from the life of Christ as though they were being played
out in his presence. The format is simple yet theologically complex,
patterned and pedagogical, inviting the believer to delve more deeply
into theological realities. The Jesuits sought intentionally to "see God
all in all things" (O'Malley 1993).

In *The Spiritual Exercises*, Ignatius develops a normative approach
to contemplative piety that has influenced not only Jesuits but people
of many faiths. Ignatius's approach is imaginative: he perceives that
a deepened, spiritual understanding of the world can be attained
through a series of set imagined scenarios. In each scenario, Ignatius
directs the viewer in what to imagine and how to apply the scene he
creates in his mind. The details of the directions are synesthetic and
bring all of the believer's physical and mental being to bear on the

event in Christ's life to be envisioned. Encouraging the cooperation of the believer with the exercise, Ignatius recommends the task of the imagination as a form of spiritual "work": "Human beings are created to praise, reverence, and serve God our Lord, and by means of this to save their souls. The other things on the face of the earth are created for the human beings, to help them in working toward the end for which they are created. From this it follows that I should use these things to the extent that they help me toward my end" (Loyola 1991, 130).

Ignatius includes animals and other aspects of creation in this project, in ways that anticipate de Sales's intentional application of animals' activity to metaphoric encapsulations of the believer's spiritual life: "The perfect, through constant contemplation and enlightenment of their understanding, more readily consider, meditate, and contemplate God our Lord as being present in every creature by his essence, presence, and power" (Loyola 1991, 133). In this way, Ignatius very clearly identifies creatures of the animal kingdom as sites of God's indwelling and presents them as tools and guides in the believer's enriching of his spiritual understanding: "I will consider how God dwells in the creatures. . . . I will consider how God labors and works for me in all the creatures on the face of the earth . . . cattle, and all the rest. . . . Then I will reflect on myself" (Loyola 1991, 177).

Along with these various kinds of Protestant and Catholic devotional manuals, we have the very distinctive *Introduction à la vie dévote*. St. François de Sales adopts the genre of the devotional manual and redefines it through a use of animal imagery. As I have suggested, devotional manuals seemed to come under less direct scrutiny from church authorities, as they were not explicitly involved in the discussion or development of church doctrine, the official teachings known as the *magisterium*. This seems to have been the case with de Sales's work.

Interest in the discussion of a deeper reality—no longer limited to or exclusively evoked by the doctrine of "signatures" but rather construed as a more sacramental sign ("a visible representation of a thing unseen") so that the fauna of faith were taken as embodying the quintessence of faith—began to circulate in some Jesuit circles, primarily because of the innovative spiritual direction of St. François de Sales, during the late sixteenth and early seventeenth centuries. De Sales's distinctiveness appears be due to his simple speech and direct references drawn from ordinary existence, designed to appeal to the reader and to be readily accessible; his increased reliance on the imagination; his uses of the senses in a very specific and intentional way; and his concretizing of this synesthetic approach through deliberate use of creatures, their activities, and an understanding and emulation of these as capable of showing the reader something about the nature of God. De Sales stresses participation in, and relationship with, the creaturely essence as one that bears the divine in some mysterious way within it, especially as it manifests its truest self in characteristic activity (such as bees hiving).

De Sales's perspective on this relational and participatory aspect of creature, creation, man, and Creator has a theological warrant, although this rationale had not been previously invoked in a method or process: Aquinas had designated *actus essendi* as that being in which all things participate, though he had never designated a creature itself as *actus essendi*. Dionysius the Areopagite had gone a step beyond Aquinas and, according to the theologian Hans Urs Von Balthasar, had spoken of how "creatures can by grace participate through the principle of 'divinization,'" though stipulating as caveat, "That in which they participate is itself precisely that in which they cannot participate, for if it were not that, they would not be participating in God" (Von Balthasar 1982, 187–88). This ontology of creatureliness relies on paradox to allow relationship but not identity with the Divine.

De Sales's use of animal imagery, consequently, is not literal or descriptive (as was Du Bartas's). It not only evokes a tangible reality or entity but suggests something to be intuited, an activity, a disposition of the spirit. Animal imagery, further, comes to be an integral component of how arguments and explanations in de Sales's devotional literature are constructed and communicated. Thus, while formerly a sort of iconographic system of code had been obtained, in which, for instance, the image of a dog equaled Christian fidelity, for everyone and in every circumstance or context, and consequently these symbols could be readily appropriated and easily interpreted, de Sales begins to examine the element of energy in movement or *animal activity* and to discern a sense of alluring mystery, or attractive and useful alterity, in animal imagery. The decoding of animal imagery no longer proceeds in an unvaryingly straightforward or transparent fashion. Instead, what is aimed at is a more complex theological understanding, or a Word about God.[4] And this Word requires a disposition of the heart, a certain inflection of the spirit and flexibility of the intellect, to be fully apprehended.

De Sales's homely, sometimes apparently irreverent, theology of creatureliness is often exquisitely attentive to the vagaries and distinctives of animal nature and is not concerned solely with how humans wish to perceive animals. A new sort of hermeneutics is invoked in his innovative attitude toward and use of *animalia:* the activity of comprehending the significance that arises from, but is not limited to and is more than, the animal itself also challenges the nature of authority, precisely because each viewer or reader will be interiorly inclined to see something individual and distinctive rather than a symbol or an element in a code.

It is ironic that the Protestant Reformation is generally credited with having introduced the liberating but also complicating notion of individual conscience or liberty of interpretation into Western theology (as each Christian belonged to the "priesthood of all believers" and could read and construe scripture for himself). However, the use of animalisms in the early modern era by de Sales certainly shows an untrammeled approach that equally cedes authority to the individual reader or viewer.

Animating Salesian Spirituality

The popular and widely used manual *Introduction à la vie dévote*, by the founder of the Salesians and master of the so-called École française de spiritualité, St. François de Sales (1567–1622), relies in large part on animal imagery to provide diverse vehicles for being in God's presence. De Sales, born in the Savoy, and educated in Annecy, Paris, and Padua, initially studied law but instead chose the priesthood and was ordained in 1593. Later, he was installed as coadjutor-bishop of Geneva, and in 1602, as bishop of Geneva, he was charged with saving the surrounding area from Protestantism, an effort in which he was very effective.

His preaching is renowned for the appeal it makes to the emotions and to the heart. De Sales believed that the bridge between man and God was constructed by man's innate capacity to love and a focus on man's will, his ability to orient himself progressively toward the divine. Gradual and kind persuasion ("douceur"), rather than coercion or forced assent, characterizes the Salesian endeavor in every way; it is therefore not surprising that de Sales should profess a view of gentle admiration for animals as God's creatures. Further, de Sales preaches sanctity in the world; he does not feel that it is necessary to distrust or flee the world (*fuga mundi*) as earlier, ascetic writers proclaimed. Within the world, and through the creatures of the world, God can be known, and a disposition of the heart that de Sales terms *bienveillance,* the desire for the good of "the other," can be cultivated.

De Sales, educated by Jesuits, through his development of the practice of spiritual direction incorporates certain key Jesuit concepts such as the *cura personalis*—he writes for, or directs, specific individuals, rather than aiming at large or anonymous audiences, and so adopts a very intimate, gently pedagogical tone. He also employs casuistry, or the case-by-case determination of ethics, morality, and spirituality, as appropriate.[5] Devotion must be exercised according to specific situation and context and will be performed differently by each individual. Spiritual direction is difficult to regulate, as it occurs outside the regular parameters of power and authority; thus animals and a new understanding of authority, the authority of the disposition of the individual's believer's heart, begin to develop in de Sales's devotional manuals. Affective experience becomes preeminent, and what better way to highlight this than through man's interactions with other creatures of God?

Animals often feature as guides or models for human spiritual conduct in the *Introduction à la vie dévote*. For instance, de Sales uses the haughty falcon who allows himself to be blindfolded and attached to the hunter's wrist by jesses as an example of how man should humble his prideful self before God: "I admired . . . how falcons returned to the fist, allowed their eyes to be covered and let themselves be attached to a perch, while men are so lacking in obedience to God."[6]

Still more significant, however, is that de Sales allots animals a place of even greater glory, for they also often represent Christ, the cosmic Christ who offers redemption and salvation to all: "Saint François, seeing a lamb lost in the middle of a herd of goats, said, 'Look how this poor little lamb stays so nicely with all those goats; just so Our Lord passed sweetly and with humility through the midst of the Pharisees.' And, another time, seeing a little lamb that had been devoured by a pig: 'Oh, little lamb,' he said, weeping, 'you represent so well the death of [the] Savior!'"[7] An immense distance has been traveled from the Thomist position of considering animals as second-order creatures, or Donne's characterization of them as "groveling," unable like man to "stand erect and contemplate Heaven," to de Sales's depiction of *animals as Christ*.

For de Sales, sanctity can and should be experienced in the world; there is no need to retire from the world, to enter a cloister, or to engage in complicated liturgy: "What is necessary is to show that Catholicism is not to be found entirely in exterior ritual" (Mackey 2010, 5, 19). The world itself offers opportunities in and through which to know God. De Sales's new approach has been described as offering to the believer an apprenticeship in spirituality through the school of the real world ("l'école du réel"; Mackey 2010, 11). His style is new, too, in terms of his characteristically simple yet evocative mode of formulation, his choice of what to look at, and the center of his interest: quotidian creatures inhabiting a real world and leading the believer's thoughts through and out of it toward a metaphysical awareness. De Sales believes that every devout person responds to God in an individual and very particular way and that the results of devotion should be according to situation and circumstance in the believer's daily life.

The sea change that seventeenth-century spirituality was undergoing, and that de Sales exemplifies, was a movement away from the head toward the heart. The paradigm was shifting away from institutionalized religion toward the practice and discipline exercised by the individual believer with guidance from a spiritual director. Further, while still endorsing an outward-looking, "active" piety, this revised seventeenth-century spirituality also advocated a piety increasingly composed of elements of contemplative practice as its point of departure.

De Sales's audience was primarily laity, often women, especially noblewomen. He wanted to write down the technique that he had developed through extensive experience as spiritual director or *confesseur*, a time-honored Roman Catholic role of providing, often, but not exclusively to a lay person, one-on-one advice, guidance, suggestions for devout reading, the opportunity to confess sins and receive correction, and a prayerful partnering on the Christian path. The premise informing a devotional manual, unlike a statement of doctrine or a catechism, is that religious experience is accessible, through affective experience, to everyone.

The devotional practice originates in *theoria physike*, the contemplation of the natural order. Note that this is not protoscientific observation, as it would be with Descartes, or even experiential interaction or philosophical rumination, as it was with Montaigne. This is a method of approaching the world and its creatures from a contemplative perspective, a spiritual practice. The assumption that de Sales makes derives from the long tradition in mystical theology, particularly that of the Pseudo-Dionysius, that God is both immanent in all things and transcendent above them.[8] This is the doctrine of *participation* or *gnosis* as unifying: God is in all creatures and yet is beyond them; the spiritual seeker must go deeper, penetrate (*optikoteros*) into this integration. (Interestingly, Du Bartas had stressed optics, the all-encompassing diving gaze. But de Sales practices a very different approach to optics, the sight of *spiritual insight*. Here his aim is not mastery or dominion is not the description but ecstatic communion through interpenetration and creaturely communion.)

Creatures may therefore lead to the divine, although they may never contain or delimit God absolutely. The distinction is that between theologians who see God in all things—that is, their subjective religious experience is strengthened when they look at a thing or a creature and, through that created being's beauty, are prompted to revere God as Creator—and contemplatives, who participate in the divine mystery by discerning God in all—the creature is in some way beyond symbol, is itself a participant in God's essence, and thereby offers something of God to the discerner: As Von Balthasar says of the contemplative Dionysius, "Things [creatures] are not simply the occasion for his seeing God; rather, he sees God in all things [creatures]" (1984, 171).

It is clear that a method or manual of contemplation is a useful way to explain this approach and to teach aspirants how to develop such a spiritual awareness of both creatures and Creator, and that is what de Sales sets out to construct. He justifies and legitimizes his approach by declaring, "Cursed are those who turn creatures away from their Creator in order to serve man's sin, but blessed are those who make it possible for creatures to serve God's glory."[9]

In some ways the reorientation of the theological endeavor to the realms of emotion and experience parallels the contemporary Cartesian reliance on experience and personal awareness of the world. But the aim is very different: the individual believer is invited to experience in a synesthetic way and, *without needing to process that information intellectually*, is invited to progress along a spiritually enriched path.

Rather than require intellectual assent, the devotional manual— especially as de Sales conceives it, through use of animal imagery— elicits instead an identification, or the rudiments of a relationship, between the figure offered for meditation (the animal) and the believer himself. It is a form of personal encounter that has as its consequence what has been called a "religion of the heart" rather than of reason or will (Campbell 2000, 36). The significance of the valuing of emotion over reason is that this, in some measure, allows de Sales to circumvent the current debate on whether animals possess reason. By sidestepping this question, de Sales is able to put his ideas forward without earning the charge of heresy that Bougeant incurs. Nonetheless, de Sales is, like Bougeant, quite creative and elastic in his doctrine.

De Sales shows nature as a conduit for grace in his *Introduction à la vie dévote* (1628). He anticipates the three principles, or basic rights of "brutes," that the Reverend Humphrey Primatt enumerates in his sermon *Duty of Mercy and Sin of Cruelty to Brute Animals*: "food, rest, and tender care," all intended by God and "provided for [his creatures], and given to them, before man was created" (1776, 147). Because he views creation in this way, de Sales is able to move to a valuing and a dignifying of the activities of creatures as more than insignificant, unintelligent, or brutish. What they do can, and does, teach us; their earthly existence is a reminder of the providential provision made for them, and for us. In a vein more suggestive and synesthetic than symbolic, de Sales lifts up nature to point to God. Johannes Kepler expressed a similar aspiration: "Lord God, through the light of nature you have aroused in us a longing for the light of grace, so that we may be raised in the light of your majesty" (1997, 36).

Perhaps the most salient contrast between Calvinist (Du Bartas and others) ways of viewing nature and grace, and Jesuit (Bougeant) and, later, Salesian ways of understanding the operation of grace on nature is to develop the contrast between a *representational* model (Protestant) and an *incarnational* model (Catholic). Du Bartas almost flattens out nature in his quest for encyclopedic thoroughness and description (even while acknowledging, of course, that this is all divine handiwork) in the *Sepmaine*. For him, in this representational model, nature *displays* grace. This is a descriptive view of the world, one akin to theological memorialism (Christ's sacrifice is remembered in the Eucharist, and God's benefits truly are offered through participation in worship, yet Christ is not believed to be *actually* present in the elements).

De Sales, on the other hand, in his *Introduction à la vie dévote*, exemplifies the traditional dictum of Thomas Aquinas that "grace *builds on* nature." His is a sacramental view of the world, in which the infusion of the Body valorizes all of creation. Transubstantiation is the theology at work here, and we find that, while the Calvinist approach to a theology of creatureliness can often be didactic in tone and pedagogic in form, the Roman Catholic approach to a theology of creatureliness—at least as de Sales articulates it—is devotional, its tone meditative and its implementation a praxis aimed at achieving a desired spiritual state.

So de Sales does not simply state the existence of animals or describe and catalogue their attributes as does Du Bartas. He assumes that all agree that, in at least some ways and circumstances, creatures magnify their Creator. But what is distinctive about de Sales's approach is that these creatures' *activities*, rather than their stereotyped (and often misunderstood) culturally ascribed *attributes*, can somehow focus and alter the spiritual disposition of humans.

De Sales's focus is, of course, inflected by the genre in which he is writing, as is that of Du Bartas. But it is also true that the two differ by cultural context and historical circumstances; new theological issues and ways of perceiving, deriving from the Reformation and the Catholic Reformation response, generate new literary strategies for dealing with animals and animality—not to mention authority—and these strategies in turn find expression, at least for de Sales, in the new genre of the devotional manual.[10]

De Sales constructs what is perhaps the first intentional *theology of creatureliness* because he explicitly sets animals to service *within* the authoritative system of Catholic belief. The spirituality that de Sales develops dwells within orthodox Catholic theology. De Sales does not revise or change dogma (as does Bougeant, whether intentionally or not), but he does, in applying doctrine, extend it, so that orthopraxis is now *spiritual* rather than merely theological. In the spiritual life, de Sales wants to make clear—perhaps in a reaction to one of the developing "heresies" of the day, quietism—that the "devout life" is active, characterized by intention and transformation, just as the Word of God is always dynamic and productive (Broekhuysen 2012). The animals de Sales refers to are very active as well, whether birds of the air, bees busily making honey, or wild animals going about their daily business.

Evelyn Underhill has described the essence of contemplative practice—an active and intentional application of the spirit and will—in this way: "As to Contemplation proper . . . thought, love and will becom[e] a unity: and feeling and perception are fused. . . . It is an act, not of the Reason, but of the whole personality. . . . The field of consciousness . . . being sharply focused, concentrates upon one thing" (1911, 329). There is much in her (modern) summation of method that de Sales practices in his meditational strategy of theatrically arranged and actualized energy, worked in and through the activity of animal figures. Through reference to animals of various sorts, de Sales creates a network of analogies, similes, and, occasionally, metaphors through which he concretizes or encapsulates the wished-for mental discipline and resulting devotional activity that will produce a particular interior disposition in an individual receptive to God in the world.

In his role as spiritual director, de Sales often dealt with people who, while they might have been culturally prominent, might not have been educated or particularly well read, especially in the areas of doctrine and faith. So his aim here was to choose a medium that would be easily accessible, understood by all, something one could intimately embrace and "make one's own." Animals provide this accessibility and immediate recognition, while also proving to be highly useful starting points for a deepening awareness of, and entry into, spiritual reality. The apparent simplicity facilitates an appeal to the heart, and through this easy acceptance a sort of self-help manual for spirituality is constructed. In sum, the devotional manual, as de Sales authors it, is meant to be simple in conception, practical in application, and affective in reception.

It is fitting that de Sales earned the title "doctor experimentalis" from church authorities, since, appropriately for his seventeenth-century context and its interest in protoscience, he relies on nature, observation of nature, and understandings derived from direct experience with animals as well as those made by authoritative sources to craft the *Introduction à la vie dévote*. Somewhat like La Fontaine, he chooses animals because of their wide and early horizon of acceptance: even children can relate to them. Yet his treatment of animals situates them profoundly in evocations of doctrine and dogma that, while never developed in a pedantic or thorough way, nonetheless teach much, in a subtle way, to the believer. His treatment of animals is anything but simplistic and respects both their particularity as animals and the concept he selects them to epitomize or evoke.

While de Sales uses a variety of natural-world examples, those involving animals are the most frequent—and, as has been stated, what is most striking about these selections is their emphasis on the animals' activity. Their activity is taken as normative, not just

descriptive, both for the animal and, if practiced, for the believer—
and thus predictive of spiritual progress. The choice of animal seems
in nearly every instance to constitute the nodal point of the noetic
thrust of the particular meditation counseled.

De Sales's method can be summarized in the following passage
from one of his pastoral letters. These letters, like his *Treatise on the
Love of God*, a doctrinal text that in many ways echoes the pedagogic
and contemplative concerns of the *Introduction à la vie dévote*, directly
address an epistolary interlocutor or a reader desirous of spiritual
instruction. In the *Treatise*, the reader is named God-Fearer, or Theo-
timus, and the *Treatise* is very much interested in illustrating and
developing aspects of human spiritual experience through reference
to animal behavior.

In this pastoral letter, which resumes many of the *Treatise*'s and
the *Introduction*'s concerns, de Sales explains the richness of apparent
simplicity and develops this concept through the twinned images of
dove and serpent. He then talks about the purpose of his devotional
project ("needfulness"). He next shows how each creature is characterized by its individuality and integrity. For instructional and devotional purposes, though, one (St. François) may intervene in nature:
he proposes a hybrid form that would elevate a specific virtue, the
beauty of prudence, while still retaining the distinctiveness of each
animal: "To tell you the truth, helpless little white doves are much
more attractive than serpents; and when we have to join the qualities of one with the other, I for my part would not like to give the
dove's simplicity to the serpent, for the serpent would remain a serpent; but I should like to give the serpent's prudence to the dove, for
it would still be beautiful" (de Sales 1960, 137). In this combination
process, reminiscent of children's flip-book creations of hybrid creatures, de Sales at first deploys Aristotelian qualities; there are specific
attributes peculiar to each animal. These attributes then become less
important than the animal's—and the believer's—activity. De Sales
shows that a positive quality of simplicity may be absorbed by the
essence of the snake, while another positive quality can be added to
the dove's beauty without altering the dove's basic nature. If there is
a positive ground to add to, additional attributes may be accrued, and

all will function positively. This is the goal of the believer's progress in the spiritual life.

Though the believer is a mere human, de Sales's premise is that within each believer there is an implanted yearning for, and even a similarity with, things divine. This affinity must be named, cultivated, and enriched. Animals, so emblematic of terrestrial existence, provide the metaphor for this process:

> It happens often amongst partridges, that one steals away another's eggs with intention to sit on them, whether moved by greediness to become a mother, or by a stupidity which mistake their own, and beholds a strange thing, yet well supported by testimony!—the young one which was hatched and nourished under the wings of a strange partridge, at the first call of the true mother, who had laid the egg whence she was hatched, quits the thief partridge, goes back to the first mother, and puts herself in her brood, from the correspondence which she has with her first origin. Yet this correspondence appeared not, but remained secret, shut up and as it were sleeping in the bottom of nature, til it met with its object; when suddenly excited, and in a sort awakened, it produces its effect, and turns the young partridge's inclination to its first duty.[11]

This doctrine of recognition (which William Wordsworth later famously developed in his "Intimations Ode," and with which Gerard Manley Hopkins worked in poems like "The Windhover," where the natural creature, the falcon, is drawn to, and even illustrates, God) is well and early developed in the *Introduction à la vie dévote*. De Sales continues by showing the anecdote's specific application to the life of the believer: "[The young partridge] is drawn by correspondence with her, which had remained hidden in the depths of its nature. . . . Thus . . . it is with our heart, which though it be formed, nourished and bred amongst corporal, base and transitory things, and in a manner under the wings of nature, notwithstanding, at the first look it throws upon God, at its first knowledge of him, the natural and first inclination to love God which was dull and imperceptible, awakes."[12]

De Sales here goes further than Aquinas; not only does "grace build on nature," but *nature already encloses something of grace* ("the natural inborn inclination"), and this has merely to be identified, teased out, and spiritually sustained. De Sales uses the images of the bird on a leash, and the hart who wears the collar of the king in his royal deer park, to show this identification and belonging. Phrases like "holding us," "links us," "gently seize and draw us," and "implanted in us" underscore the intense correspondence between natural creature and Creator:

> It serves God as an anchor by which he may the more gently seize and draw us to himself, divine goodness holding us in some wise linked by this sentiment with himself, as little birds by a string, by which he can draw us when its pleases his compassion to have pity on us. It is a mark and a memorial of our first principle and Creator, to whose love it moves us, giving us secret intimations that we belong to his divine goodness, even as harts upon whom princes have had collars put with their arms, though afterwards they cause them to be loosed and run at liberty in the forest, do not fail to be recognized by any one who meets them . . . as being reserved for him.[13]

Surpassing the medieval Catholic notion of nature inscribed with signs and symbols of God's intentionality, the images of bird and stag display *relationship*: the harmony between man and God, facilitated through the dynamism of the animal anecdote, that preexists man's awareness of it.

Nature is the privileged theater for this doctrine of correspondence, and the theology of creatureliness is what enables it to be discerned in the devotional manual. De Sales's view of nature is a very strong and possibly unprecedented positive valorizing of *animalia* as already participating in the nature of God. His catalogue of animal references, in both the *Introduction à la vie dévote* and the *Treatise on the Love of God*, is extensive and varied, rivaling—although treating in a very different way—even Du Bartas's encyclopedic plethora of references. To name only a few, de Sales speaks of horses, sheep, tortoises, falcons, peacocks, silkworms, bats, roosters, pilot fish, wolves, bulls, oxen, ostriches, nightingales, bees, stags, owls, serpents, coral, foxes, lions, kids, ewes, oysters, chameleons, dragons, finches, larks, hounds, cicadas, pelicans, storks, and the phoenix. Always his focus is on the animal's activity and how that may be construed as illustrative of a path that the human seeking further knowledge of God should take.

A Salesian Spirituality of Creatureliness

Certainly de Sales was not the first religious writer, or mystic, to use animal imagery. The Sufi poet 'Attar described the theopathetic state, when the self is utterly merged with God, as one of being "like fish in the sea" of divine love ('Attar 1924, 130). Meister Eckhart declared that "to [the soul] all creatures are pure to enjoy, for it enjoyeth all creatures in God, and God in all creatures" (1909, sermon 3). St. John of the Cross at times evoked birds, and fish, and other creatures to describe the soul's dependency on God. The English mystic Richard Rolle compared his spirit to a nightingale: "It is said the nightingale to song and melody all night is given, that she may please him to whom she is joined. How muckle more to Christ my Jesu should I' sing, that is spouse of my soul by all this present life, that is night in regard of clearness to come" (Rolle 1914, 2:7). St. Francis of Assisi preached to and thereby tamed the wolf of Gubbio.[14] St. Rose of Lima was overheard singing spiritual songs at evensong to and with the birds: "At once the little bird began to sing, running through his scale to the highest note. Then he ceased, that the saint might sing in her turn. . . . Thus did they celebrate the greatness of God, turn by turn, for a whole hour" (Underhill 1911, 415). St. Teresa described how, in the phenomenon called "recollection" that prepares for mystic vision, the senses gather in during prayer "like bees which return to the hive and there shut themselves up to work at the making of honey."[15]

So how is de Sales different? He himself is aware that his use of natural-world referents is innovative, and he acknowledges this in his preface: "These are indeed the same [materials as those found in other books on the natural world] that I present here, reader, but I preset and arrange them in my way, which is different."[16] What is it about seventeenth-century context, and perhaps the contemporary Catholic mentality, that predisposes him to make such frequent reference to animals?

First, he uses them *systematically* and in a *spiritual*, rather than a philosophical or theological, way. Through them, he exalts nature as capable of lifting man to God. Indeed, grace lifts nature beyond itself, as the twinned examples of pearls and butterflies attest here: "Just as certain pearls live in the sea without ever taking on even a drop of salt water, and the butterflies called 'pirautes' fly through fire without burning their wings, even so a strong and steady soul can live in the world without becoming worldly."[17]

De Sales uses a variety of natural-world examples, most prevalent among them animal references, and what is most striking about the activities of the animals is that they are taken as *normative*, not merely descriptive and, if practiced by the believer, as *predictive of his spiritual progress*. That is, the customary dualistic divide between world and heaven, flesh and spirit, animal and human, is transcended and bridged by God's grace. Each has something to offer the other, de Sales avers.

This is a *sacramental* view, but with a personal or *individual* inflection. Much as in medieval Roman Catholic theology, for de Sales the divine is believed to be revealed in a space-time continuum in specific places, objects, creatures, stories. These realities act as openings onto the holy. Yet, as Michel de Certeau has shown, in the aftermath of the Wars of Religion, the seventeenth century began to question authority in many profound ways (1995, 116). That century of conflict had introduced an element of doubt about monolithic certainty and had fostered a relativizing mentality, and the resulting multiplicity of confessions fractured the former (ostensibly) homogeneous nature of man's certainties. Further, while the medieval view had stressed the cohesion of macrocosm (God) and microcosm (man, at the head of nature), Descartes split theology from science, thus challenging the chain of similarities and resemblances on which the view of the world as *imago Dei* had rested.

With the consequences of the Protestant Reformation, and its concomitant focus on the interior action of God and His Word over and against the former emphasis on the action of external grace, seventeenth-century theologians begin to speak more of the possibility of individual access to God. The devotional manual was a preeminent tool in this *ascesis*. Essentially, to some extent the *authority of inward experience* displaces (although de Sales never seeks to *replace*) external authority as the basis for religious knowledge. With affective experience displacing tradition and authority as the real heart of the religious life, the way is clear for a more individual and personal appropriation of belief.

De Sales's *Introduction à la vie dévote* was revised and then reprinted as many as forty times and translated into English, Italian, Latin, Spanish, and German. The *Introduction* adopts the literary fiction of consisting of a compilation of letters written to one person, Philothée, the feminine form for "Lover of God," and, later, Philotheus. Each Philothea and Philotheus remains individualized for de Sales, epitomizing the spiritual director putting into practice love guided by imaginative insight into particular and specific spiritual circumstances. At the same time, de Sales gives the generic name of "God lover" (Philothée) to *all* his readers, those whom he will take by the hand and guide spiritually through this enchanted garden of peaceable beasts.

The *Introduction* has an easy, simple, and adjectively emotional style and tone. A complete program for holiness in the world, sanctification in, with and through God's creatures, is explicated in it, as though in intimate conversation, and in stages evolving logically one out of the other.

The approach is simple, clearly patterned, and highly accessible. It entails five parts: the determination to move beyond a "désir vague" to a "résolution ferme et entière" to inhabit a spiritual life; an acceptance of sacraments and prayer as the two preeminent ways to come to God; the practice of virtue; warnings against traps that nonbelievers might place in the path; and an invitation to "retire into one's inmost being."[18] This final phase is perhaps the most important, for it displaces the theater of influence and authority from the external world—and, indeed, from the institutionalized church—and resituates it within the individual believer's heart. An exclusively affective experience may now occur.

De Sales brings in animals to act also like what some would today call "spirit guides": their actions and activity concretize visually certain recommended states of mind, heart, or spirit and specific daily-life actions that the believer should take. For instance, de Sales creates a scenario of spiritual direction between a nightingale and her young: "Fledgling nightingales learn to sing with adult nightingales. Just so, by frequenting saints, we will learn better how to sing God's praises and how to pray."[19] The animal suggests the meditational practice counseled, as the animal activity is, at the one and the same time, accurately represented (singing) and *figuratively redirected* (singing praises and praying) for the spiritual seeker.

As bishop, de Sales feels it is incumbent on himself and other bishops to devote themselves to others' spiritual direction. In the early Christian Church, he reminds his reader, that was a primary episcopal charge. The present-day church has moved away from such a pastoral focus. This is a very significant reforming statement on de Sales's part and shows why he should be considered a revisionist figure in seventeenth-century Catholicism. It means that the most important activity in which church authorities can engage is not that of serving the institution but that of reaching individual hearts: "Bishops in the old days and the church fathers were at least as devoted to their pastoral calling as we are, and even so they did not turn away numerous seekers who came to them for guidance; it is a heavy responsibility to have the spiritual direction of individual souls, but it is also a heart-warming ministry!"[20]

And how is the bishop to do this? De Sales immediately commends the process of the devotional manual with an animal example:

It is said that a tigress, having found in her path one of her cubs (which a hunter had left there so that she would be distracted while he made off with the other cubs), picks that cub up, no matter how plump he might be, and carries him safely back to their den, and she does this speedily, as though her load were lightened by natural [motherly] love. How much more will a fatherly heart take under care a soul in which he discerns a great yearning for perfection? He will carry that soul in his very heart.[21]

The animal is both the pretext for, and the illustration of, the devotional scenario; elsewhere, de Sales pledges, "I will lead his dear lambs to the saving waters of true devotion."[22]

Later eras have accused de Sales of a somewhat saccharine style. But what is operative in his manual is not sentimentality but the endorsement of a newfound permission to apply the imagination on every sensory level, to enable the seeker to visualize scenarios through the medium of other creatures whose simple, easily imitated, activity points toward the Source and illuminates a spiritual truth. Reason and intellect do not need to be invoked; the believer can have an intimate, immediate, individual, affective experience of the spiritual reality represented in the animal micronarrative. The authenticity of the spiritual path is attested to by the seeker's willingness to emulate those creatures that rise to God rather than to belabor scripture with intellectual inquiry or doubt: "Eagles, doves, and swallows fly often, quickly, and very high. Just so truly devout people fly up into the heavenly heights often, quickly, and very high. In short, the authenticity of the spiritual life will be verified by the agility and the promptness with which charity takes effect in our hearts, and with which we act on her promptings."[23] Not sentimentality but emotionality set to the very practical service of spirituality characterizes the *Introduction à la vie dévote*.

Continuators of a Theology of Creatureliness: Devotional Manuals and *Animalia* after de Sales

De Sales had many contemporary continuators and commentators. Chief among them, Pierre de Bérulle, born in Champagne in 1575, was educated in Paris and, beginning in 1592, at the Jesuit college of Clermont. He was ordained chaplain at the royal court in 1599, and his official role called for him to be polemicist against the Protestants during this intense period of Roman Catholic reform. Like St. François de Sales, he frequented the circle of Madame Acarie (later Marie de l'Incarnation). His Christocentric focus led him to introduce the order of Carmelites in France and to participate in the reform of secular clergy called the Oratoire de Jésus, which brought him—like Bougeant, but for different reasons—into conflict with the Jesuits: the education that the Oratoire offered competed with Jesuit schools.

Bérulle himself was eventually brought up on charges of heresy by the Carmelites for being insufficiently mystical in his construal of the vow of servitude. His focus on the concrete and the practical was in line with de Sales's emphasis on elements of real life and daily life in spiritual practice: "Spiritual progress happens very simply in the context of daily life. . . . The life of the Spirit manifests itself through actions. That is why very base and ordinary actions such as sweeping, washing dishes, serving at table . . . are perfect in God's eyes. . . . Now, this simplicity can be found only in a continual attentiveness to God."[24] Indeed, Bérulle was much in contact and correspondence with de Sales, whose writings had a great influence on Bérulle's thought, also very sacramental and incarnational. Bérulle's sophisticated understanding of the path to God became very popular and very prevalent in seventeenth-century Europe.

The method that Bérulle advocated for meditation shows similarities with de Sales's devotional model. While Bérulle is more verbose and more obviously emotive, he takes similar steps to those of de Sales, which Bérulle enumerates here, to foster the individual experience of the divine: "Those who contemplate *a rare and excellent object* are pleasantly surprised by the astonishment and admiration they experience at the first sight of that object, even before they recognize in detail the particularities of the subject they are contemplating. Furthermore, this astonishment, which appears to cause a weakness in the soul, gives it strength and vigor. For the soul draws strength from its weakness, *elevating itself to a greater light and to a higher and more perfect knowledge*" (Bérulle 1995, 36). The "object" is akin to the animal in that contemplation of it has a strong effect ("astonishment" and "recognition"), causes a revision of foregoing categories, and produces a primarily emotional response ("admiration") that is also—in terms of the world and spirit ("for the soul draws strength from its weakness")—somewhat paradoxical ("causes a weakness in the soul, gives it strength and vigor"). The final effect is a spiritual distance traversed, an "elevati[on]."

Further, Bérulle's theology of the Incarnation views God as the unity encompassing all of creation; creation reveals this unity in plurality, which makes of God what Bérulle calls "une unité sociétaire." It is difficult not to see in this plural perspective the in-gathering of clusters of birds, herds of cattle, prides of lions, just as le père Bougeant identifies most animals, following Montaigne, as social by nature. Bérulle says that Jesus himself is an entire world; therefore, presumably, all of creation is incorporate in him and therefore has value: "For just as in creation there is mixture [of substances, divine and creaturely], there is also admixture in the Incarnation, which results in a divine composite."[25] For Bérulle, as for traditional Roman Catholic theologians, creation shows God's imprint; *all* the world is collectively inclined toward God. Modern-day commentators have even likened Bérulle's theology to that of Teilhard de Chardin, calling it a form of theological "écologie."[26]

Further, since sin is defined as a turning away from God, the opposite of incarnation, which insists on relationship (man-God in Christ), and since animals are construed as not sinning (this perspective is maintained in Bougeant's thesis), animals must in some way be *closer* to the divine than is flawed humanity. So, in Bérulle's theology, the purpose of the Incarnation is redemption (*réparation*), and fallen man is incapable of achieving this for himself. By grace he may be raised, and he is, in fact, destined for grace. It is this quality that sets him apart from all other creatures. But the progressive divinization that Bérulle determines is man's destiny is a benign and cooperative one, beneficent toward other creatures: "This new man, who lives on earth, is a new creature. . . . He is a divine composite of the creaturely order and the uncreated, the one is deified by the other . . . We love the earth because God's Son was incarnated not in heaven but on earth, and this earth is honored with his presence, marked with his footsteps, watered with his blood, honored by his mysteries."[27]

This creaturely and redemptive, indeed divinizing, anthropology, if pushed to its logical limits, seems to suggest that animals have no need of grace because they have not sinned and that consequently they are more pure and closer to God. Such an understanding turns traditional dominion theology on its head. This understanding may, indeed, illustrate how Bérulle interprets the rationale undergirding de Sales's reliance on animal imagery to facilitate devotional practices.

Père de Caussade, also a Jesuit and much influenced by de Sales, wrote extensive and important correspondence and published an affective devotional manual entitled *The Sacrament of the Present Moment* (1741). "The inspiration of [his] doctrine is derived primarily from St. Francis de Sales" (Foster 1982, viii). Like de Sales, he uses animals and other elements of nature to focus the believer's attention and to indicate right living and right belief: his goal is to "look at life and see all creatures, . . . their meaning; . . . to moreover see the living God in all things" (Foster 1982, viii). For instance, the discussion of sanctification is summarized by an image of the silkworm's activity:

> Exist, little worm, in the dark confines of your narrow cocoon, until the warmth of grace hatches you out. Then devour the leaves offered you, and, forgetting the quietude you have abandoned, surrender yourself to this activity, until divine nature stops you. Alternatively active and passive, by incomprehensible transformations, lose your former self, manner and habits, and through death and resurrection, assume those which divine nature will herself choose for you. Then spin your silk in secret . . . by surrendering yourself you will be inspired to spin silk that princes of the church . . . will be proud to wear. . . . Who ever would have guessed what nature makes of a silkworm unless they had seen it! Only give it leaves, nature does the rest. (Caussade 1982, 101)

Caussade's image highlights the activity of the silkworm, interweaving aspects of its creaturely existence with themes of transformation drawn from theological reflection, such as the Resurrection, and also demonstrates a more than passing interest in the natural sciences with its carefully observed account of the silkworm's life cycle.

Like de Sales's emphasis on the activity—rather than the attributes—of animals as facilitating devotion, Caussade's method emphasizes process, movement, and flow and values each moment of the believer's day and entire life: "God speaks to every individual through what happens to him moment by moment. . . . No moment is trivial . . . since each one contains a divine Kingdom, and heavenly sustenance" (Foster 1982, xiii, xix).

It can be seen that while the Protestant Du Bartas paradoxically penned the *Sepmaine* from the standpoint of man as the *summum* of creation, omitting the typical Calvinist focus on man's depravity after the Fall, and in this way working from an assertion of dogma, de Sales, displaying Catholic understanding of the efficaciousness of good works and man's eventual and progressive perfectibility in Christ, differs from Du Bartas in that he writes, not from a standpoint of dominion and domination, but from the perspective of devotion and discipline. Those who continue his theology of creatureliness, such as Bérulle, epitomize this same tendency.

For de Sales, the believer can be coached and gently brought to set himself right with God, in the inner space of his heart, through the examples offered of fellow creatures, and in this process a theology of creatureliness is developed where the creatures have equal standing with man: "My dear Lover of God, let us unite our hearts to these spiritual and blessed souls. Young nightingales learn from their elders to sing. In the same way, by the intercession of saints we shall learn how to sing God's praise and [also] to pray better."[28]

Both the animal model and the human believer are set *in relationship* in de Sales's text, and this relationship is crucial: they enter into a preexisting community ("let us unite our hearts to these"; "by the intercession of saints, we shall learn"), and a threefold interaction ensures, entailing pedagogy ("Young nightingales learn from their elders to sing. In the same way, by the intercession of saints we shall learn how to sing God's praise and [also] to pray better"), a unitive understanding, and a salubrious imitation of animal by human. In the devotional anecdote just cited, de Sales has encapsulated the practice of spiritual devotion.

De Sales's influence extended to other realms besides that of devotional or meditational literature; it is also apparent in cultural productions having to do with animals, theological issues, and the interaction between the two. For example, the Jesuit artist and polymath Athanasius Kircher certainly handles some of his grandiose, intricately detailed illustrations of periods of biblical history in terms of the sorts of "memory theaters" that Ignatius suggested and that de Sales develops by emphasizing the meditational tool of animals' activity and movement.

In Kircher's illustration of Noah's Ark, for example, we can see this phenomenon at work. Kircher often uses animals as figures to suggest a doctrinal teaching, as is the case with the rutting stallions on "Noah's Ark." Strikingly, the two horses are the *only* creatures so engaged and would seem emblematic of the original sin that necessitated the Flood. By standing at stud, they may summarize a theological teaching. Yet, while their act suggests a dogmatic point, the horses cannot conclusively be said to embody it. Animals remain outside doctrinal norms, which they may or may not be illustrating. That is, they retain their strangeness and mystery for Kircher. Unlike medieval Catholic depictions of animals, their presence is evasive and elusive; their function is not clearly coded.

The two horses' act of copulation while in the belly of the salvific vehicle, the ark, shows creatureliness as a part of, even a necessary component to, the soteric scheme. Kircher doesn't try to alter or edit natural animal behavior. What he provides is, in fact, a "God's-eye view" of nature. Like de Sales, this seventeenth-century Jesuit makes the depiction of the animal activity valuable *in se;* it also has potential value in encouraging the imagination to envision its theological significance and daily-life application. It might, for instance, prompt mediation on rampant sexuality and sin leading to the Flood.

In the illustrations of Kircher, nature *as it is is* taken up into Noah's Ark. Paula Findlen has termed these "ark" spaces for the neo-Ignatian imagination "theaters of nature" (1994, 10). The ark is a figure of salvation. Thus, when it does invite or facilitate meditation, the Kircherian illustration acts as the kind of imaginative theater that St. Ignatius of Loyola recommends in the *Spiritual Exercises* and that St. François de Sales animates with creatures in the *Introduction à la vie dévote*: the reader (for Ignatius and de Sales) or viewer (for Kircher) enters into the depiction, imagines himself within it, and ponders the spiritual revelation suggested by it.

There is no need to edit, alter, or reconfigure the nature of nonhuman animals; they are acceptable and lovable to God as they are—in all their nonhuman particularities of existence—as evidenced by

Kircher's detailed drawing of animals copulating while in the ark. This is a brave rebuttal to Descartes's refusal to consider that animals have speech, form societies, have worth, experience suffering. The decision to incorporate animals into theological texts and illustrations, to feature them as privileged mediums in the act of salvation through enhanced spirituality, is a robust Roman Catholic riposte—from a handful of contemporary Roman Catholic thinkers more drawn by spirituality than obedient to dogmatic authority—to Cartesian proto-scientific insistence that animals are mere automata or machines.

LE PÈRE BOUGEANT'S HERESY

Animal Societies, Languages, and Souls

An honest view of animal minds ought to lead us to a more profound respect for animals as unique beings in nature, worthy in their own right. The shallow and self-centered view that sees what is worthy in nature as that which resembles us seems vapid and petty by comparison. . . . We define true intelligence and true feeling in human terms, and in so doing blind ourselves to the wonder of life's diversity that evolution has bequeathed earth. The intelligence that every species displays is wonderful enough in itself; it is folly and anthropomorphism of the worst kind to insist that to be truly wonderful it must be the same as ours.
—Stephen Budiansky, *If a Lion Could Talk*

I would be tempted to say that the animal [is] a Philosopher. . . . Think of a big fat, whiskery cat sitting calmly in a corner. . . . He never gets distressed by the things that bother us. . . . Are [human] Philosophers any more wise [than he]?
— Guillaume-Hyacinthe Bougeant,
Philosophical Amusement upon the Language of Brutes

In the film *Ridicule,* a portrayal of salon culture, the character of the Abbé, "lion" of his salon and virtuoso of verbal improvisation and witty repartee, grandiloquently proves the existence of God before the king and his assembled courtiers through a series of cleverly reasoned plays on words. When the king rises to applaud these punning pyrotechnics, the Abbé, caught up in the adulation and swept away by his own arrogance, brags to the king, "Mais, Sire, je pourrais tout aussi bien preuver le contraire!" His boast that he could just have easily demonstrated the nonexistence of God is met with shocked silence and an immediate fall from favor. His Majesty, a devout Catholic, is not best pleased.

The Abbé has made the crucial misstep of forgetting that, despite his brilliant mind and rapier wit, he is bound and held by the cultural conventions of his Catholic context. In many ways, le père Bougeant was guilty of the same oversight. He, too, was bound by the conventions and the generic expectations that he had formerly met—to great praise and enthusiastic readership—throughout Europe: theological rectitude and respect for church authorities. The latter were no more willing to grant him liberty of interpretation or to cede him license for originality than they were to concede that animals could communicate, or than the king was willing to let the Abbé's boastful blasphemy pass unpunished.

Bougeant failed to acknowledge that he was confined, just as were his contemporaries, in ideological frameworks of social, cultural, and theological construction. Although he may have attempted to dodge such censure by labeling his work an *amusement* and calling it *philosophique* rather than religious, his previous writings, and his reputation, had created expectations that his readership retained. Much as the culture in which Bougeant lived imposed on animals a framework that anthropomorphized or reductively defined them by human standards, the Jesuit hierarchy imposed its definition on Bougeant of what was acceptable, pitting his perspectives against authoritative church teaching.

Just as sensory perspectives drawn from the natural world have illuminated previous chapters, two senses are foregrounded here, sound and sight, as the argument for vocalized (but also gestural) animal language and communication is framed by the sign language of deaf-mutes. The dawning realization in the seventeenth century that deaf-mutes were not handicapped or disprivileged but every bit as intelligent and capable of communicating as other, more apparently advantaged humans, is paralleled by Bougeant's insistence—building on Montaigne, but also on his own experience and observation—that animals, formerly construed as lacking reason and the ability to interact through language, similarly possess intelligence, form cooperative societies, devise plans for work, and communicate among themselves within and between species. These were bold claims, flying in the face of traditional Aristotelian reasoning, according to which plants had vegetative essence, animals possessed sensitive being, but only humans possessed rational souls. Bougeant's claims were therefore taken by church authorities as revolutionary and dangerous, tantamount to the Abbé's arrogant assertions described above.

Born in Quimper in 1690, Guillaume-Hyacinthe Bougeant entered the Society of Jesus in 1706. He professed formal Jesuit vows in 1724. A historian, for many years Bougeant taught rhetoric and the humanities at Caen and Nevers. He subsequently lived in Paris, where he died in 1743. Bougeant published numerous works under the name le père Bougeant, among them the important and controversial labor of love entitled *Amusement philosophique sur le langage des bêtes* (1739/1954). Although the work was stunningly successful in the world of the salons that he frequented and was widely disseminated in Europe—it was translated into German, English, and Italian—the *Amusement* was ultimately condemned by the Vatican for heretical speculation concerning the existence of animal souls.

While Jesuit thought was still significantly influenced by Aristotelian concepts in the early modern era, some seventeenth-century spiritual publications penned by Jesuits, and other tracts of Jesuit authorship, showed an important divergence from such teleological thinking. When that was the case, the reaction of contemporary authorities could be extreme and severe. Bougeant ran afoul of the Roman Catholic authorities in part because he diverged from Aristotelian constructs and claimed that *something more* (which, unfortunately for him, boldly for his era, he called a "soul": *anima*) was inherent in the animal.[1]

Ironically in the *Amusement* Bougeant seems to have been applying, among other methods and arguments, the Ignatian technique of "spiritual exercises," the visualization process developed by St. Ignatius and practiced by the Jesuits and upon which St. François de Sales drew and elaborated for his *Introduction à la vie dévote*. In many ways like both Loyola and de Sales, Bougeant took an approach that was not definitive or denotative, but suggestive and connotative.

In many respects Bougeant was a most doctrinally correct Jesuit. For instance, among his other publications are theatrical plays, several of which satirized the contemporary heresy within the Catholic

Church of Jansenism (Bougeant called the Jansenists "Les Quakres [sic] français" in a 1732 play bearing that title). Further, Bougeant had authored a theological treatise concerning the Eucharist, as well as a widely used catechism for religious instruction that actually remained in use until 1900. His orthodoxy in these matters notwithstanding, Bougeant was briefly exiled in 1739 as a result of his affirmations about animals influenced by Eastern ideas of metempsychosis, and he was required by the Catholic hierarchy to publish a retraction of his assertions before he was allowed back into France (Harrison 1993, 540). Although his historical studies, notably of the Thirty Years' War, were deemed magisterial, his treatise on animals and their spiritual lives was judged heretical.

What was the impulsion or conviction that led him to write this book? The religious angle appears to be crucial: Bougeant's version of Roman Catholic belief, as articulated in his understanding of how Jesuits lived out their calling in God's creation, led him to consider animals as equal to humans. The belief that God had placed his fingerprints on each small part of creation, that he revealed himself in and through his creatures, seems to have influenced Bougeant in his love for animals. If this was the case, then why did his contemporaries and fellow Catholics reject Bougeant's characterizations of animal life? What did they find heretical about his arguments?

One of the problems was that for church theologians worried about the correct phrasing and transmission of dogma, praise of animals that tended toward an assertion of animal souls was tantamount to an attack on Christianity and Aquinas's assertion that animals had no souls.[2] On the other hand, the church had no problem with Descartes, who upheld Christian doctrine in this respect. In his letter to the Marquis of Newcastle, Descartes explicitly stated that were animals to think as humans did, they would then of necessity have an immortal soul—and this notion, of course, was "not likely."[3] Descartes had directed much of his energy to combating Montaigne's influential espousal of animals' language and ability to signify.[4] And Bougeant went one step further than Montaigne: he upheld the idea of animal soul and developed a complex and convincing theory to prove this.

Bougeant alarmed the authorities because he seemed to vacillate on church teachings, equivocate about theological and philosophical systems that denied capacities to animals, and leave room for the individual reader to discern the truth for him- or herself on the basis of the evidence presented and the use of his or her "common sense" (*bon sens*). For the Catholic hierarchy, such flexibility and freedom in interpretation was tantamount to the excessive liberties that Protestants had taken with the *magisterium* and with church tradition. Too much room for error! One historian has noted that "it is somewhat surprising, to tell the truth, to find, between Bayle and La Mettrie, a religious writer spreading materialist and sensualist ideas without correcting them. Bougeant's crime—if it was indeed one—is that he propagated heresies"[5]—not just one heresy, to the minds of the authorities, but many.

It seems that a separation of ways developed within Roman Catholicism itself, a profound difference of opinion—if not doctrine—in which the spiritual literature, generally less bound by dogma, less supervised and scrutinized than explicitly theological texts, and thus often more open to personal inflections of belief, began to express the notion of a shared *anima* between humans and animals, as in the writing of St. François de Sales. But in Bougeant's case this latitude for personal expression did not obtain. Although he purported to write for a popular and unordained audience, the *Amusement* was not a devotional tract, and Bougeant's reputation as a highly regarded theologian got him in trouble with authorities, who expected him to produce theological exposition rather than popularized philosophical speculation.

This illustrates the persistent and tenacious character of the imposition of authority, and its shortsightedness: after all, Bougeant is doctrinally correct in the *Amusement* in that he elaborates on Aquinas's dictum that "grace builds on nature"; the problem, however, is that in discussing animal nature, he refuses to distort what he sees that nature. For him, animal nature has been misconstrued and misunderstood theologically. In trying to describe and examine animal nature as it actually is, in his eyes, Bougeant goes out on a potentially heretical limb. The heretical swerve occurs through Bougeant's assertion of *difference*, rather than a safe reduction to similarity (as in La Fontaine's anthropomorphizing anecdotes), between humans and animals. Once that difference has been postulated, animals need to be portrayed and scrutinized in their own right, as *their* nature really is.

Although continuing to work with a characteristic vocabulary and (despite the "philosophical" demurral) within his customary theological mental system, Bougeant affirms the notion of animal soul. He does not dodge it, as does Descartes, whose theory of the animal-machine differentiates more between body and soul than between animal and human: as Stephen Budiansky has remarked, "The soul—possessed uniquely by man—was to Descartes a matter beyond scientific scrutiny, but the body—possessed by both man and animals—was fair game for science" (1998, xxv). But Bougeant wants to talk about his belief that animals possess souls—the very human-animal analogy that Catholic theology will *not* condone.

La Fontaine's Fables and Fallacies

Some of the impetus for Bougeant's work had to do with the contemporary interest in protoscientific phenomena. At a time when Descartes was experimenting on animals and asserting that they were "mechanisms" without souls, the debate raged furiously in salon culture as to whether this was in fact the case.

The philosophical debate over the possibility that animals might reason, might possess souls, might indeed be very similar to humans, began at least as far back as the sixteenth century, as already discussed, with Montaigne's "Apologie pour Raimond Sebond" and other assertions scattered through his *Essais*. Montaigne tells stories and anecdotes to praise animals for their intelligence, their reasoning capacities, their self-government, a language peculiar to them, and their moral discernment. Montaigne claims that man demonstrates his own hubris when he purports to be superior to animals—in effect, to *other* animals than himself. Similar thinkers to Montaigne, known as the "thériophiles," go so far as to assert that, if man is the sole possessor of reason, this capacity is in fact a curse, since reason prevents man from knowing happiness.

In 1732, for instance, a contemporary of Bougeant's named Morfouace de Beaumont wrote a poem illustrating precisely this point and extolling the superior contentment of animals. De Beaumont's "Apologie des bestes" characterizes animals as saying, "The present moment is enough for us. Our sole aim is to enjoy ourselves. Concerning the obscure future, we have no worries."[6] And the 1770 *Dictionnaire des gens du monde* defines the human condition as unhappy by virtue of the ability to reason.[7]

One of Bougeant's contemporaries, the poet and fabulist Jean de La Fontaine, penned the famous "Discours à Mme de la Sablière" and another fable entitled "De l'âme des bêtes" in which La Fontaine upholds a position similar to Bougeant's, asserting that animals do have souls. His reasoning differs somewhat from Bougeant's, but the notion of animals with souls appears, in the case of both authors, to be influenced to some extent by Eastern theology.[8]

With much speculation in the air concerning the possibility of animal souls, a primary preoccupation of both learned societies' discussions and more popular venues, such as the journal *Les mémoires de Trévoux*, essentially three positions were bruited about concerning the nature of beasts in seventeenth-century salon culture. The Cartesians upheld the conviction that animals did not suffer during experimentation because they had no souls and no sentience; they were a form of machine moved by gears and inner workings but not by emotion or awareness. The *gassendistes*, among them La Fontaine, reacted strongly against this position and maintained various notions of a hierarchical chain of being, from atoms on up, in which every living being had value, sentience, and experience intrinsic to itself and perception valuable *in se* (Rochot et al., 1955). Interestingly enough, nearly all of these cultural discussants had received a Jesuit formation. And then le père Bougeant, himself a Jesuit, eventually cast out as heretical, believed that animals had a form of reason, their own language, and a soul.

Before we look at Bougeant's argument in detail, it is instructive to see what La Fontaine has to say concerning the "nature of beasts."

While frequenting the celebrated salon of Madame de la Sablière from 1672 to 1678, La Fontaine conceived of a new form of fable that he called the "fable philosophique." This generic innovation enabled him to expand upon themes, to amplify in a more discursive way some of his portrayals of humans as animals, and to situate these in relation to issues under contemporary discussion. These fables are more sophisticated in argumentation, necessarily so, since La Fontaine's interlocutors included men of science such as Gassendi, the mathematician Roberval, astronomers, doctors, and world travelers. La Fontaine's philosophy in these fables shows the influence of Gassendi; it exemplifies epicurean moral and metaphysical philosophy and his belief in the goodness of nature and the display of Providence in nature. In this respect, like Gassendi, La Fontaine vigorously refuted the Cartesian notion of "animaux-machines." His "Discours à Mme de la Sablière" (*Fables*, no. 9) takes on Descartes's theory point by point.

La Fontaine's argument takes the form of a didactic poem, a sort of philosophical polemic in which he ironically explains the Cartesian position and then deconstructs it. The *gassendiste* and the Cartesian positions are clearly polarized, with characterizations being presented as the opinions of "us" versus "them": "So they say that animals are machines; that everything within the animal is done by mechanisms and without choice: no feeling, no soul; everything within the animal is body alone."[9] Not only does the Cartesian stance relegate the animal to the status of insensate matter; it further reifies the animal by viewing it as a kind of machine, a watch ("montre") that always ticks along in a regular fashion, blindly and with no aim ("aveugle et sans dessein"); one can open up its case and inside all that will be seen is wheels and gears.[10] This machine has, of course, been well designed, and each part fits with and moves another.[11] But despite its intricacy and clever design it is only an insentient machine.

La Fontaine then presents the opposing side: "selon nous," the Cartesians are wrong when they say that there is no passion, no will, no emotion in the animal's experience; they tell us not to deceive ourselves when we see the animal appearing to act out of pleasure or pain, since this simply is not so. But, La Fontaine avers, according to us, "c'est autre chose." La Fontaine pokes fun at Descartes, who, considering himself the pinnacle of God's creation, is able to produce only the rather self-evident dictum, "Je pense, donc je suis": "'Look, I say, at how this author reasons: 'Superior to all the animals, children of God the Creator, I possess the gift of reason, and I know that I think.'"[12] La Fontaine says that Descartes denies that animals can reason, yet La Fontaine states that, if they do not reason or reflect on their acts, they certainly do think, and he illustrates this assertion with a minifable, an anecdote about a stag being hunted in the forest. The stag, exhausted by the hounds and the hunting horses' harrying, persuades a younger deer to run out into the fray as a decoy to divert the pack and to spare the older stag. This successful tactic can be assessed only as "que de raisonnements"; demonstrating what looks a lot like logical thinking, the stag plans a strategy, executes this ruse with cooperation from another with whom it presumably had to communicate, and arrives at a favorable outcome.

La Fontaine fights science and Cartesian lists of logical proofs with storytelling, and this is a persuasive popular technique. Instead of proofs, he proffers examples of other such anecdotes and then concludes: "Now try to convince me, after hearing such a narrative, that animals don't reason."[13] Finally, La Fontaine states that animals must have at least as much ability to think as do children to whom we ascribe the power to think from infancy, yet of whom we do not expect the same capacity for reasoning or self-awareness that an adult possesses.[14] La Fontaine's argument strikingly anticipates Peter Singer's canny and controversial exaggeration of a similar perspective in *Animal Liberation*, when he says that if we are going to deny reasoning and sentience to animals so that we can experiment on them, we should equally carry out experiments on infants and the mentally challenged (1975, 121). La Fontaine maintains that animals do feel, experience, perceive, and make lower-level decisions and that a monkey thinks, and therefore, he is. La Fontaine makes an explicit and gently mocking equation between Descartes and the monkey, just as earlier he situated Descartes somewhere between an oyster and other men on the scale of intelligence.[15]

La Fontaine and Bougeant are notably similar in their opposition to what they see as Cartesian reductionism. But they also have many significant differences. Unlike La Fontaine, Bougeant is concerned not to anthropomorphize. La Fontaine's fables rely on an anthropomorphizing strategy, offering easily understood pedagogic models for children as well as engaging fables about human foibles for adults through the cipher of animal figures who act—and even, in some of the engravings, look, and sometimes dress—much like humans. As a result, many of La Fontaine's assertions about animal habits are inaccurate. His fallacies have been pointed out by scholars.[16] The important point, however, is not his errors about animal nature but the fact that he obviously considers such erroneous statements to be insignificant—even as he offers the fables as instructional texts for children. What seems to matter for La Fontaine is that he convey a similarity between animals and humans, in such a way that the animal nature hides what at times can be some fairly outrageous, or even subversive, statements about absolutism (Chambers 1991). That is, the animal nature is a mask or smoke screen. La Fontaine appropriates *animalia* for human ends and purposes. His focus is always primarily human nature.

Bougeant's Beasts

Not so Bougeant. In fact, in an interesting twist, Bougeant was also the author—anonymously, as he feared further censure—of a work entitled *Lettres philosophiques, sur les physiognomies*, a treatise that asserts that a person who looks like a particular animal will possess characteristics of that animal. Bougeant reverses La Fontaine's method here: rather than make animals resemble and represent people, Bougeant makes humans resemble and act like animals. To do this, he must hold to an understanding of animal nature as somehow more primary, strong, or fundamental than human nature. And, indeed, in another tract, *Observations curieuses sur toutes les parties de la physique*, Bougeant asserts that the instincts of animals are more sure and reliable than human reason (1739/1954, 33). Clearly, he was coming down on the anti-Cartesian side of this debate.

So Bougeant, unlike La Fontaine, was preoccupied with representing animals as accurately and as "naturally" as possible, and thereby showing a likeness between humans and animals based on experience and observation. To do this, he had to try to circumvent Christianity, because church teaching maintained the inferiority of beasts to man and upheld humanity's right to rule over the animal kingdom (Scully 2003).

The *Amusement philosophique sur le langage des bêtes* is a self-styled popular work. "Amusement" is not a customary title or recognized subgenre, but it is in the same category as "dialogue" or "discourse" or "exposition" or even "account." Therefore, Bougeant intended his work for a secular audience, most likely those who frequented the Parisian salons at which he was a literary lion. Much of its argument, at least in the first part, the section devoted to investigating whether animals possess souls, is also directed against Descartes. What is odd is that, while the title and tone are secular, and those implicitly addressed in the work are lay people, the argument is *essentially theological*. And this hybridity of the text was what proved to be Bougeant's undoing and what earned him the label of heretic.

A popularizing tract, the *Amusement* could have been written and received simply as a sort of pastime, a frolicsome venture into the impassioned contemporary debate about the nature of animals. Bougeant's criticism of Descartes was not in and of itself troublesome to church authorities, although most were far more comfortable with Descartes's position than with that of the *gassendistes*. Bougeant's assertion that animals have feelings and reactions similar to ours and that it makes good sense to assume that they therefore possess some awareness of these emotions was not far removed from La Fontaine's argument, and La Fontaine was not reproached for his stance. But La Fontaine was not a Jesuit, and unlike Bougeant he was not the author of serious theological texts. Bougeant was advancing a theological argument cloaked in a secular costume. Because of the gravitas of his other, much-admired works, the argument he advanced in the *Amusement* was doubly worrisome to church authorities.

The comparison with La Fontaine in terms of subversive speech is instructive. La Fontaine often resorted to fables as a masking device that enabled him to voice criticisms about arbitrary exercise of authority.[17] Louis XIV could be a dangerous and autocratic patron, as La Fontaine had learned when his powerful friend, the king's minister of finance Nicolas Fouquet, met his downfall at the hands of his former patron. La Fontaine guarded against a similar outcome by veiling his thoughts with quaint anecdotes and folksy narratives. When he penned "Le loup et l'agneau," for instance, he took care to identify the wolf with rapacious courtiers rather than with the power of the king, his actual target. Through subterfuge, sarcasm, and irony, La Fontaine was able to make some subversive statements. To hear them, one must read between the lines, look beneath the ostensible meaning (*sub-version*). Because La Fontaine was careful, and because the causes he took on remained in the secular realm, he dodged retaliation.

Bougeant in the *Amusement* also adopts a mask, though his self-camouflaging strategy is much less well developed or consistent than La Fontaine's. Bougeant poses as an anonymous "Auteur" in his text, pretending to have heard another say the words he himself is actually uttering. But this mask is fairly transparent. He also addresses his argument to a young lady, in this way minimizing the boldness of his arguments, since its ostensible intended recipient was fairly insignificant socially, at least for the period. His destinatee is meant to be amused; the tract is characterized, initially, as "one of those discourses that one just tries on without forethought . . . and without other aim than to enliven the conversation; a pleasantry."[18] Further, Bougeant purportedly writes at her behest; she decides to take his argument seriously and urges him to prove it, and this posture diminishes somewhat his authorial responsibility.[19] And he's out in the country, not in the city, just relaxing and discoursing "sur toute la nature." Or so he says.

But, unlike La Fontaine, Bougeant is not subverting the system; rather, he is *reformulating* it, actually erecting his own system at the expense of accepted church teaching. And Bougeant goes the distance that Descartes never seeks to travel and that La Fontaine refrains from traveling: Bougeant asserts that animals had souls. One of the insurmountable problems here, for Roman Catholic theologians, was that were animals to have souls and/or reason, their very existence would be blasphemous, as they did not have any duty to God. According to Thomist theology, every creature fits into his distinct place within the

natural order, but only man has a duty to God. He owes this obligation precisely because he is empowered by reason, and motivated by
his soul, to discern and perform such a duty: he was created to give
glory to God (Linzey and Regan 1988, 24). The assertion that animals
had either reason or souls implied that God had made a mistake in
creating them.

Bougeant's very creative but troubling solution to this dilemma is
to assert that animals are inhabited by demons who refused to serve
God and who, as a result, are condemned to transmigrate: "Metempsychosis: that is, at the moment of our death, our souls pass into a
body, be it the body of a man or of an animal, to begin a new life there,
and this continues in this way until the end of time. This system,
unacceptable where humanity is concerned, and of course forbidden
by the church, works beautifully concerning animals in the schema I
am proposing."[20] As a result, animals do also speak a kind of language,
since they were once the obedient souls of reasonable men. It seems
that Bougeant wants to have a radical argument within an acceptable
theological framework but cannot think outside conventional theological categories. Trying to stay within the Catholic fold, Bougeant
argues that, if animals have souls, those souls will, by definition, be
immortal and have free will; animals then have access, presumably,
to either heaven or hell, neither of which eventuality is provided for
in Catholic theology. But if they have *demons,* in the parallel place of
souls, then they are free of the obligation ("Devoir") toward God that
all created *souls* have (Bougeant 1739/1954, 18).

Bougeant's task, then, is to find a way to give beasts a (demonic)
soul without contravening the principles of religion. To do this, he
draws on church authorities but radically rereads them, interpreting
scriptural passages in a new way and thereby implicitly criticizing
what he finds to be inadequate or inaccurate scriptural commentary
and exegesis.[21] By annotating authority he is altering it. Bougeant
continues to situate his argument in reference to traditional theological understanding: "The church teaches us that demons were
rebuked from the moment that they sinned, and they have been condemned to burn forever in hell."[22] But he now finds a loophole into
which he can insert his new interpretation: "But the church *has not*

yet decided whether they suffer *at present* the torment to which they are destined."[23] This differs from the situation regarding human souls: church teaching is that the soul is separated from the body at death and usually sent immediately either to heaven, hell, or purgatory. The church has not made an official pronouncement concerning what happens to demons, Bougeant points out, and, because church authority has not yet resolved the issue of whether demons suffer the pains of hell at present or will more likely do so in the future, Bougeant has room to maneuver ("on peut donc croire"): there is no tradition, in this respect, with which he must comply.[24]

This is how Bougeant believes he can remain within orthodoxy while developing an entirely new doctrine: "I find the basis for my system within Religion itself."[25] And, just in case, he cites a few authorities who he thinks might agree with him.[26] He states all this while still using the cover of the anonymous Auteur. Clearly, he remains worried that his approach may be too bold; he anticipates the charge of heresy that is eventually leveled against him, saying that one may say to the Auteur, "Monsieur, votre proposition est formellement hérétique."[27]

Bougeant continues to argue his case, stating that, in the absence of definitive church teaching, he is entitled to conclude that demons do not yet experience the pains of hell, although they have been irrevocably condemned to it, and he quotes scripture to this effect (Bougeant 1739/1954, 27). The significance of this lacuna, and of Bougeant's belief that demons are currently at liberty in the world, is that he can then continue to develop his theological reasoning, stating that because God has a purpose for everything he does not allow these creatures to remain inactive and instead infuses their spirits into various animals: "In order to not leave these [demons] idle, God has sent them into various parts of the world . . . and placed them in beasts of every kind."[28] Bougeant even finds an ingenious explanation for plagues of locusts or swarms of flies: these insects are caused by God to proliferate when there is a surplus of demons needing a new dwelling place.[29] In this way, Bougeant arrives at what he feels to be a perfectly acceptable Catholic version of metempsychosis: "In such a manner, . . . I have no trouble conjecturing how, on the one hand, demons can tempt us and, on the other, how animals can think, know, feel, and have a spiritual soul, without contravening church teachings."[30]

The argument of usefulness is one he also makes elsewhere, in a nontheological vein, asserting *l'utilité* as the ultimate natural and reasonable criterion for the existence of animal languages.[31] These useful and reasonable limits are also salubrious, since, held to these perimeters, animals do not, according to Bougeant, suffer from the emotional and psychological sins, such as pride and jealousy and avarice, that plague humanity: "In the dictionary of their language, they know only how to express their desires, and their desires are limited to what is purely necessary for their preservation."[32] This practical and pragmatic aspect of animal existence in fact elevates them above human passions and whims: "They may not have our advantages, but they certainly don't have our failings"; if they are don't speak a theoretical or philosophical language, they are also less inclined to sin or err.[33] Language, to summarize the theological view, is marked by the Fall for man; no use of language is recorded in the Bible during the prelapsarian era, Bougeant concludes, and the superiority of animals is, in this respect, implied: "Besides, just think of how abusively men use the ability to speak that nature has given them! Think how many errors and lies are the normal subject of our conversation! So much extravagance and so many trifles, so much ill-saying and backtalk!"[34] The demon argument would seem to imply the contrary, and seems negative, at first view, where animals are concerned: If animals are demons, would they not be expected to lie? But, Bougeant asserts, beasts always speak truthfully ("disent toujours vrai"). How can this be? Bougeant is not saying that animals are demons, or even that they have demons, but rather that they are inhabited by demons developed within another being or entity. He implies that what is infused into the animal, according to his theory, is *human* evil. In this way, animals come to be seen as superior to humans, in that the evil or sin is not of their origin or making. They are simply the repositories as man's sinfulness works itself through the universe.

Further, Bougeant is probably not all that serious about his demon theory: he is fairly dismissive about proving it. He needs to make the argument about the transmigration of demons into animals because, in his system, it is necessary that animals have a form of *soul,* so that they can have intelligence and language. This latter topic is his real interest: "You ask me if I seriously believe that animals speak. Yes, my lady; I believe very seriously that animals speak and understand each other as well as we do, and sometimes better than we do."[35] He therefore sets up an equation in which man possesses body plus soul, while an animal possesses the parallel structure of body plus demon: "Just as man is soul and body organized together, so each animal is a demon united to a body."[36] This demon, however, is a damned soul— but *not yet:* some process—and, consequently, some progress—is still possible, though unlikely, since the demon takes up a new life in a new animal host; therefore, a final pronouncement cannot yet be rendered as to salvation or damnation.

Further, the ways that animal communication proceeds, and its effects, are valued highly—to the detriment of humans. Where language in particular is concerned, Bougeant makes many criticisms of humans. This proves troubling for church authorities. *Language* is the important issue for Bougeant ("la principale question"), and he gets to its possibility through the juggling he does with demons and souls. Bougeant devotes much time to proving and examining the details and functioning of animal language, once he has asserted its existence. When it comes to the issue of communication among animals, Bougeant drops his mask: no longer the pseudonymous Auteur, he speaks as "je."

He makes it clear that he wants his readers to *do something about and with animal language,* namely, to observe animals carefully and then to compile for themselves a dictionary of animal words and speech: "If you want to possess the dictionary of the language of animals, observe them in different circumstances while they are showing different emotions, and as they generally have only one expression for each feeling, you will quickly be able to compose your dictionary."[37] Significantly, Bougeant seeks to convince a woman, more socially— and certainly more theologically—marginalized, even in the salon culture of the late seventeenth century, rather than a male interlocutor. The fiction of the woman reader is more preceptorial, more hierarchical, a less problematic site for the transmission of revisionist authority, and woman is closer to the status of animal than is man in the contemporary *mentalité*.

This praxis will then connote acceptance of his theory. In this interaction between Bougeant and his fictive female reader a sort of confessor-confessee relationship develops in which Bougeant exerts precisely the sort of authority to influence the reception of unorthodox ideas that the church was afraid he would wield. This intimate relation comes closer to the scenario of spiritual direction within which St. François de Sales works. And yet, because Bougeant is seeking to communicate knowledge—both experiential and *intellectual* (*theological*)—the latitude for the exercise of the individual imagination that church hierarchy seems to have allowed the genre of the devotional manual (concerned with *spiritual* information) is not granted to him.

In another twist on the issue of authority and animal matters, the effect of the dictionary project will be to exile the woman reader from the salon; she will now want to haunt the woods and fields and talk with the animals in a pleasurable new Eden.[38] In short, valuing animal speech will have consequences: the woman will be akin to animals and will frequent their dens and lairs. No such fate is envisioned for a male reader. Bougeant is surely aware that (male) church authority will reject at least some of his conclusions. So while Bougeant leaves the countryside to promulgate his theory in Paris, if he successfully convinces his (female) reader of his theory, she will leave Paris and take his place in the country. Understanding animals, though gratifying, may result in exile from one's culture and peers—as Bougeant himself discovered.

Bougeant takes on Descartes by referring to his dictionary project as one that will follow a very precise and detailed "method" ("sur le modèle que je vous ai proposé"), Bougeant's *own* method.[39] Contrasted with the assertion "Je pense, donc je suis," Bougeant's assumption is "Animals make sound, therefore they speak": a counter-Cartesian proposition that Bougeant now sets out to substantiate. Man must divest himself of any cultural or theological notions of superiority, any mandate that other creatures' worth can be assessed only by him: "It is necessary to absolutely do without any notion of sentence structure or grammatical construction. . . . The reason for this is simple: such terms express abstract and metaphysical notions that animals don't possess."[40] He admits that "we do have to transcribe their expressions using phrases that we write in our way," but this is a concession to humans' inadequacy, not a description of any deficiency in animal speech: "All things considered, what does it matter whether animals say phrases personified and composed in our human way, as long as they make themselves understood by each other?"[41]

Montaigne had stated a century earlier that animals possessed a language; he had asserted that animals speak and that we simply do not understand what they have to say. To some extent, Bougeant follows Montaigne's reasoning when he responds to his fictive female interlocutor, who protests to him that she loves her dog and cannot conceive that it might be a demon. His response is that we construe our companion animals to be what we want or need them to be; we shape them after our perception of them and our projection of ourselves, but in fact we do not recognize their true nature. He says that our love for animals is unreasonable.[42] This form of self-serving anthropomorphizing leads the owners of pets and lovers of animals to public outcry when horses are whipped, parrots mistreated, dogs abused; they ask, What harm has this ignorant animal done, that it should be so treated? Bougeant now has the answer for them, and it is his own theologically derived response: "Religion teaches us the reason for this: it is that they were born sinful."[43] (Although it seems so, this assertion is not incongruent with his theory's contention that animals' sin is not original but "infused"; it is of human, not animal, derivation—since demons, in Bougeant's theory, transmigrated from humans before ending up in animals). Human sinfulness is the explanation. Bougeant enumerates a list of cruel animals, among them cats, predatory beasts, monkeys, and even dogs. They do not choose to be cruel, he allows; rather, they are "necessités à faire le mal" in this theological system he has developed.

Man is born innocent and distorts his own nature by turning away from God. But animals, Bougeant argues, have this perversion infused into them when it departs from a human body. He explains, "Accept the theory I have devised and everything makes sense. The souls of animals are rebel spirits [demons] guilty before God. This sin in animals is not a sin that originated in them; it is a personal [human] sin that corrupted and perverted their [animal] nature throughout."[44] Animal sinfulness thus derives directly from *ours*.

Bougeant is going much farther than Montaigne here. For one thing, the terms he uses, such as *demon*, are theologically freighted and derived. And his reasoning is ultimately presented as forming an ancillary part of church teaching, as resolving a question that has been left unanswered (and thereby implicitly criticizing church authorities' failure to have resolved this issue earlier, to have left a theological lacuna). Finally, the ultimate effect of his system is to create a similarity and a parity between man and animal, such that they are capable of similar experiences and emotions because they possess similar natures.[45] This homology rests on a negative likeness, but even if beasts are inferior to humans—by reason of deriving from that which was created pure spirit but fell to a corrupted and demonic state—Bougeant argues, their similarities are greater than their differences. And, ultimately, he actually implies a superiority of animal to human.

Contemporary Roman Catholic theology, concerning Christian anthropology, is that man alone possesses language. God created man superior and gave him speech to set him apart. God endowed humanity with the ability and skill to construct artificial languages. But only infrequently in the Bible is any mention made of animals communicating with themselves or with humanity. In earlier legends, such as those collected in Voragine's *Légende dorée* or the tale of St. Francis preaching to the birds, some animals are reputed to have spoken or to have communicated with men. But it is understood that these are exceptional and miraculous occurrences, special divine dispensations given to highlight the sanctity of a holy man rather than to exalt or magnify the capabilities of the animal. What Bougeant's system proposes is entirely different. First of all, it is precisely that: a system. He develops a whole manner of thinking about animals' language, reason, and souls that seems, if a bit unusual, plausible and coherent. Second, there seems to be nothing about his beliefs that gives God glory. A feminine and dominant nature usurps the place of the Divinity rather too much for the church's liking in Bougeant's thought: "Let's turn to nature to find the proof of my theory."[46]

Bougeant, again following Montaigne, who praised animal self-government and graciousness, asserts that many animals, such as beavers, are made to live "en société." And social order requires communication: "Plus de communication, plus de société." Bougeant creates a mini-anecdote in which he depicts a group of beavers cooperating and designating tasks in order to build their dam: "Some go to get wood, others to find clay that some carry by turning on their backs and making their bodies a sort of sled that others pull to the place where [the materials] are needed. There, one beaver acts as a mason, another as foreman, and another as architect."[47] In such micronarratives, Bougeant focuses on the beneficial social interactions among animals facilitated by their speech. If animals are fallen demonic souls in his theological theory, nature certainly shows them to be industrious and of value—every bit as communicative, cooperative, and productive as humans can be.

Although Bougeant's text is little read today, what is known of his work is this sort of description; this particular passage is what endears him to animal rights activists. The beaver mason, the beaver builder, and the beaver architect all coordinate their activities, embodying the proof of what Bougeant has been affirming: that animals can and do communicate, at least as effectively—if not more so—than humans.[48] There is order and harmony in this small society, and language is the factor that creates order. Any rational being can see this, Bougeant argues, and rationality perceives rationality: there is a reason for what these beavers do and for how well they are able to do it together. He deliberately contrasts the beavers' productive activity with the biblical Tower of Babel, a manmade construction that, because of arrogance, was doomed to fail and was toppled as the consequence of divinely engineered breakdown in language: "Isn't it obvious that an endeavor so well organized and so well carried out must be because those animals were talking among themselves, and using a language in which to communicate their thoughts? Remember, my lady, what happened with the Tower of Babel: that's what happens to any society that does not have a language."[49] It would appear that God is on the

side of the beavers, if not of the humans, for he allows their construction to endure. The animals do not seem to have the problematic
emotional states that typify humans, such as the hubris that toppled
the Tower—another implication that Bougeant actually finds them
to be superior to humanity in some respects. Church authorities also
deemed this suggestion suspect.

While some might protest that what motivates the beavers or the
wolf pack is instinct and not language, Bougeant protests that so much
intricacy is required for what animals do singly and together that the
word *instinct* is used dismissively and reductively by humans who are
not capable of perceiving the complexity of the animals' communica-
tions. Indeed, animals are our pedagogues and we should properly
be their pupils. "Since we say [here] that beasts have knowledge, why
say that instinct is useless? Why ascribe to unknowable instinct something that might be the simple result of their knowledge, and since it
is effectively knowledge that enables man to do similar things, why
couldn't that also be the case with animals?"[50] Enumerating animal
skills and wisdom as did Montaigne, Bougeant describes how storks
teach men how to make and use antiseptic rinses, pigeons show how
gravel can be an aid in digestion, sparrows give spiders to their young
as emetics, birds craft their nests with a multitude of skills. Even solitary animals, as opposed to sociable animals, possess a form of language, he maintains, "for if some animals can talk, that means all of
them do"; even oysters and snails can speak.[51]

While animals might not possess an actual language, which he
defines as the entire collection of possible words, Bougeant asserts
that they possess what he calls "parler," a series of words pronounced:
"We call language something that differs according to the different
peoples [who speak it]. It is certain that animals speak, even if we
cannot recognize their language. But isn't it possible that [without
using our language] they speak and are understood just as truly?"[52]
The rhetorical tool of the negative interrogative, so much affected by
preachers in the pulpit subtly to compel agreement, is here typical of
Bougeant. Bougeant resorts to this technique frequently, going on to
inquire of his reader, "When you really think about it, isn't it the case
that animal language seems limited to us only because our language

is too diffuse?"[53] In another extended mini-narrative, Bougeant again uses the negative interrogative in an account of how wolves hunt together "avec beaucoup d'adresse." They are so clever that they know how to stake out one wolf, creating the appearance that he is menacing a flock of sheep, to deceive the shepherd into attacking that solitary wolf while the others then attack from an entirely different hiding place: "Now, doesn't such a well-developed plan show that the . . . wolves conferred together . . . and how is it possible to confer without speaking to each other?"[54]

At times Bougeant forgets his theological argument and seems to credit an omniscient and maternal "Nature" with endowing animals with these capabilities: "Let us conclude, therefore, that since Nature, who always acts so wisely, made animals to live together in societies, Nature also gave them every thing necessary to do so and, as a result, gave them the ability to speak."[55] Bougeant now situates the context for his writing act: he is writing while away from Paris, out in the country, surrounded by "toute la nature." He also defines his method, which will be to search out in nature the examples needed to prove his conviction that animals do possess language.[56]

But the nature of which he speaks is not a neutral or a secular nature; rather, Bougeant immediately theologizes it, recalling animals of the Bible, the serpent in the Garden of Eden, Balaam's ass, and so forth. Any pretense at secular discourse is here undercut by the religious parameters of the text. Further, he situates his discussion within the format of the expository or homiletic narrative. He will address three questions: Do animals possess self-awareness ("connaissance")? If so, can they speak? If so, in what manner do they speak?

Bougeant grapples with the issue of authority in this matter. He will not do as classical authors or even Renaissance writers like Montaigne did: that is, compile citations from other authors and authorities to strengthen his case. Instead, he makes an appeal to personal experience. This is a strategy much more employed by contemporary Protestants than seventeenth-century Roman Catholics, who generally seek to legitimize their viewpoint by situating it in reference to the church fathers and to tradition.

But Bougeant also wants to take on Descartes the man personally, so this is how he proceeds. Rather than appeal to church authority, Bougeant seems much more concerned to appeal to the common man: his example is calculated to alienate others from Descartes's point of view. "You have a beloved dog, and you believe she also loves you. I defy any Cartesian to convince you that your dog is only a machine."[57] Calling on emotion, sentiment, the attachment between animal and master, Bougeant takes direct aim at the Cartesian concept of *animal-machine*: "Now, if Descartes's opinion were true, you would see how crazy everyone would be who thought himself to be beloved of his dog, and who loved his dog with knowledge and feeling."[58] Labeling Descartes's theory "opinion," Bougeant evokes the early modern concept of Opinion, one often associated with madness, delusion, or mob rule.[59] Further, "opinion" clearly contrasts with "authority," for "opinion" can mean heresy or error in a theological sense. Bougeant also demonstrates that Descartes's error is in reasoning not from proof but from conjecture. Descartes claimed that God *could have* made animals as mere machines. This perspective would have been acceptable to church authorities, for it in no way undermined the omnipotence of God.

But Bougeant goes on to play with the same kind of conjectural logic, asserting that, by that same reasoning, all the men around him may also be merely machines, since God *could have* made them thus, and since Bougeant has as little access to their thought processes as he does to the inner minds of animals. Yet just because God was able to do so in either case did not mean that he did. And given the structures of homology between men and beasts, if an animal seems to be communicating something, seems to be feeling something a man could also feel, why not consider this a likelihood? "When I observe someone speaking, reasoning, and acting as I do, . . . I believe that the man I am observing possesses principles of knowledge and abilities similar to mine. Well, animals are, in comparison to us, very similar."[60] Bougeant thus sidesteps theological argument to appeal again to personal experience and to the knowledge that can be gleaned from personal observation. This move resembles certain authorial strategies of late sixteenth- and early seventeenth-century Protestant writers, and it is certainly one of the factors that troubled church authorities when they read the *Amusement* (Taylor 1989). *The self is set up as authoritative:* the very definition of heresy (Parris 2010).

Further, Bougeant's argument, like Montaigne's, has relativistic ramifications. While he judges man, Bougeant suspends judgment of animals. Indeed, he refuses to judge them; they are exempt from judgment because any evil that inheres in them is human in origin (infused, demonic), not animal. He requires his reader to assess them as we would an alien yet equally worthwhile civilization, like that of Montaigne's cannibals.[61] Allowing what is known and acceptable in one's own society to be the determinant of what we will acknowledge or applaud in another society is an error. On these lines, as noted earlier, he argues that animal languages, though different from ours, should be recognized as true means of communication.

Bougeant's reasoning about animal language leads him down the path taken by Montaigne: cultural relativism is implicit in the conclusions both men arrive at. Bougeant asserts that, while animals may not speak a language that we would recognize as such, it is nonetheless a true method of communication: "We call language something that differs according to the different peoples [who speak it]. It is certain that animals speak, even if we cannot recognize their language. But isn't it possible [without using our language] that they speak and are understood just as truly?"

The church teaches that animals do not have souls. Contradicting church teaching with his own experience and observation, Bougeant relies on what he himself can see, know, experience, and deduce: "I see a dog running when I call, caressing me when I pet him, trembling and fleeing when I threaten him, obeying me when I order him to, and giving every sign of possessing various emotions"; Why, then, he asks, should I conclude that the dog has no feelings, sensations, emotions, or soul?[62] And since there is this observable sort of call-and-response between animal and human, how could one not arrive at the conclusion that language exists peculiar to each species (since many animals, such as dogs, live in packs or "societies" and thus need language to communicate among themselves) and also that communication is possible *between* differing species of animals? He points to how human reason functions and concludes that animals, too, possess a form of this capability. The words *donc* and, later, *puisque* and *par conséquence* underline a causality in the reasoning and underscore the logical tenor of his argument, while the first-person plural form of the verb invites the reader to agree with Bougeant: "So let us agree that [they possess], as a result, the ability to speak, whatever their language may be."[63] Bougeant does not yet try to define what this animal language consists of; he is first concerned simply to persuade the reader of its existence.

He continues to advance his argument by emphasizing its plausibility due to the similarity between human and animal action and response to events and emotions: "Everything speaks in an amorous beast as in a man in love. Everything expresses his passion: his gestures, his voices, every movement."[64] In describing what is essentially "le gestuel," the animal's body language, Bougeant differs from La Fontaine, who reduces animal language and motion to a human form and metaphor. Bougeant likens what the animal experiences to a similar phenomenon in humans but maintains the distinction between those two experiences: what the animal undergoes is similar to but different from. The animal experiences in its own idiom (*"sa* passion; *ses* gestes; *sa* voix; *ses* mouvements"). Nonetheless, he insists, these embodied manifestations are all semantic parts of a form of language (*"tout* parle").

The language of animals arises in circumstances like those that produce human language: Both live in intercommunicating groups, both experience emotions and feelings that generate utterance. But the language of animals is different from that of humans in that it appears more limited ("borné") than ours.[65] Yet this limitation is not a lack; rather, animals' language is situation appropriate. Significantly, after using the adjective *borné*, Bougeant proceeds to expand on animals' language capacity; rather than accepting their speech as "limited," he goes on to characterize it as extensive and adequate.[66] This is a limitation that is no curtailment but is instead right, fitting. and sufficient, "more or less perfectly proportioned to their needs."[67]

Bougeant takes the example of birds as a template for understanding the speech of other animals.[68] He makes this selection because of birds' variety of speech elements, the superior quality of their articulation, the relative ease with which humans can become aware of birds' speech ("le plus sensible pour nous"), the existence of patterns of intonation and accent, and the quality of phrasing that can be discerned in their speech. Enumerating various kinds of birds, including the blue jay, the crow, the magpie, the duck, the turkey, and the owl, Bougeant invites his reader to acknowledge a system of analogy underscoring the similarity between the speech of humans and bird speech: if humans aren't sure what birds are saying, the humans should imagine what they themselves would say, and that, he unhesitatingly asserts, will be "exactly what the bird is saying!"[69] He also maintains that, contrary to popular wisdom, which argues that animals cannot experience joy or reflect on it and lack the awareness that would make them laugh, humans are not the only species able to laugh; animals do in fact laugh "très-bien à leur maniere."

In fact, Bougeant asserts, maybe the reason animal speech appears nonexistent or inadequate to man is that our own system of communication is so scattered and imprecise ("trop diffus").[70] The language supplies what the animals need, it provides the tools they require in their animal experience. Bougeant stresses that this is not a paucity, a failing, or a shortcoming. In this, he leaves himself vulnerable to the charge of heresy, since traditional theology holds that man is "made a little lower than the angels," excels by virtue of reason and language, and has dominion over the beasts.

Not only is the language of animals as extensive as is necessary for their use, but it is the failing of humanity, a lack on man's part, that he is unable to discern its richness and significance. Regarding birds, for example, some may protest that they repeat the same thing over and over, yet besides easily noticed differences, such as speed, pitch, and length of song, "there are very likely many others that we do not notice, for lack of being able to understand their language, but which the birds understand among themselves perfectly well."[71] The "limit" here is set on man's adequacy of perception, not on animals' intelligence.[72] Bougeant imagines a scenario in which a man who has been deaf since birth but is suddenly being granted the ability to hear will listen to what other men are saying and—uninstructed in the

existence, sound, or purpose of vowels, consonants, and syllables—
will mistakenly believe that they are incessantly repeating the same
word or words.[73] This is an erroneous assessment, yet "that's exactly
the sort of judgment we make concerning bird song," Bougeant
maintains.[74] It is humanity's shortcoming that it fails to perceive the
beauty, utility, and complexity of birds' communication, for instance:
"We talk all the time every day to animals, and they understand
us perfectly well. The shepherd makes his sheep understand him,
cows understand everything a little peasant girl tells them, we talk to
horses, dogs, birds, and they understand us. Animals speak to us in
turn, and we [can] understand them [if we try]."[75]

Human communication has another flaw: it can be misleading,
exaggerated, and full of deceit. "Compare, if you will, what we call a
lack in animals to what we deem an advantage in our speech: rhetorical developments, metaphors, hyperbole, complicated sentences—
and you will see that, where birds are concerned, their speech is
always simple and true, while in human speech there is too much
wordiness, and even downright lies."[76] Human communication is
complicated and goes beyond what is needed, appropriate, or right;
the series of nouns and adjectives with which Bougeant describes
human speech are laden with negative freight: *pretend, amplifications,
hyperboles*. And it is difficult not to hear—if dangerous to hear—the
contortions and serpentine convolutions of the devil's stereotypical
twisted speech in the term *entortillées*. The communication of animals
is innocent and pure ("du simple & du vrai"); they do not lie. What
men construe as an advantage ("avantage") or an asset is, in reality,
a defect ("défaut"), which characterizes all of humanity, as Bougeant
underscores through his use of the first-person plural pronoun, *nous*,
and adjective, *nos*. All of mankind is marked by this flaw, a sort of
secular and semantic Adamic fall from grace, the "original sin" of
language misuse, from which animals are exempt. This is risky terri-
tory for Bougeant to enter.

Directly after constructing this dichotomy between the purity
of animal speech and the mendaciousness of human language,
Bougeant explicitly mentions original sin. He openly walks onto theological ground. Before man sinned, he avers, he could speak with

animals and understand them when they spoke clearly among themselves; thus it was man's sin that led to the breakdown of interspecies
communication. Animal languages are unmarked and unchanged by
the Fall, while human speech bears the stains of sin: "The language
of animals and birds is in no way subject to change or variation [as
our speech is]. Nightingales and finches speak exactly the same languages they spoke before the Flood."[77] Man's fall from grace disrupted
a divinely ordained linguistic harmony: "Paradise was populated by
animals who spoke among themselves and who expressed themselves in an intelligible way [sensément]."[78] Sensément suggests that
prelapsarian creaturely communication was reasonable—that it possessed the very quality that church authorities point to as unique to
humanity.[79] It would appear that humans lost the ability to speak with
animals by humans' own fault. Refusing to acknowledge the coherence
of animals' language systems, they then further sinned by denying
that animals communicated. Their sin resulted in the mendacious
aspect of human language—a taint from which animal speech is
free. Not only is this statement clearly critical of humanity, it is also a
revisionist theological argument that Bougeant is sketching out, and
one that directly contradicts church teaching.[80]

Difference and otherness, hardly conventional categories for theological discussion—unless it is to label such perspectives heretical
—become touchstones in Bougeant's text. Animals represent them.
And so superior does Bougeant deem animal to human speech that
he recommends that a universal language be founded on the model of
animal communication: "Shouldn't we, rather, hope . . . that humans
will use [the animal] model to create a universal language that will be
understood throughout all creation?"[81]

Another form of difference and otherness on which Bougeant
draws to elevate the status of animal speech is that of the deaf-mute:
"Put together two entirely deaf people. Their union will never last unless
they have a way to communicate facts and to express their needs. Two
sparrows without any sort of language would find it equally impossible to coexist [without language]."[82] The seventeenth century was very
much interested in the possibility of communication between those
born deaf and dumb, and some religious began schools to help those

disadvantaged in this way. Bougeant was ahead of his time; in France, it was not until the Enlightenment that people stopped scoffing at the possibility of a form of speech among such people. But, like animal speech, the communication of deaf-mutes is very effective, Bougeant argues, just in a different way from ours: "Gesticulations, gestures, movements that create a very intelligible language and that make up for [*font . . . un supplement de*] vocalized speech. . . . Are these not speaking actions?"[83] Bougeant shows that the situation of animals is analogous to that of the *sourd-muets*. Indeed, because such speech is shown to form a "supplement" to human speech, the latter is represented as, in itself, inadequate. Traditionally the church propagated the belief that a child's deafness resulted from God's punishment of his sinful parents. Consequently deaf people were excluded from taking part in religious worship and were deemed lesser, uneducable, flawed human beings, on a level with "imbeciles"—and with animals. For instance, for many years "deaf and dumb" people were not allowed to make a will or to inherit property from their families.

For creatures such as deaf-mutes or, Bougeant goes on, fishes, reptiles, and insects, who appear to be silent or incapable of language, we should do as the readers of Montaigne's essay "Des cannibales" must do to grasp the gist of the communication of the "other": we need to turn matters on their head, discern the truth behind appearance, and liberate ourselves from our stereotypes.[84] These other forms do, in fact, constitute other languages. While we speak with lips and hear with ears, animals have homologous somatic structures that we need to acknowledge as well: "Why should they not be able, using a mechanism similar to our tongue or gullet, to produce vibration and delicate . . . sounds which . . . can then be understood?"[85] Other creatures make sounds that are produced not by voice but by the movement of body parts, as in the case of crickets rubbing a membrane, yet this is "l'équivalent de l'expression vocale."[86] In another culturally relativistic argument similar to Montaigne's assertion that cannibals who wear no breeches nonetheless have ethical and moral laws and strong social relationships that the scandalized Europeans seem incapable of valuing, Bougeant shows that crickets and wasps and grasshoppers produce language that man is unable or unwilling to deem communication. The "otherness" stressed—even admired—in Bougeant's argument enters into direct conflict here with orthodox authority: "Everything speaks when we so desire. Imagine a people of mutes. Do you think that they would be unable to be understood among themselves, that lacking our words and our sentences, they could not make up for this lack by using cries, gestures, looks, and facial expressions? Then let's apply this analogy to animals. They do not have [our] language [*le langage*], but why should they not have [their own] language [*un langage*]?" (Bougeant 1739/1954, 65–67). Bougeant's continued use of the negative interrogative again gently steers the reader toward envisioning matters his way, and his distinction between "le langage" and "un langage" shows the arbitrary superiority that humans attribute to themselves, without recognizing the communicative capacities of others.

Bougeant asserts that it is both unreasonable and contrary to nature ("il est impossible dans l'ordre de la nature") to deny that animals possess the ability to communicate. His argument proceeds from the particular to the general; as one species can speak, so can others; as humans can communicate, so can animals.[87] And his conclusions, he maintains, are founded on "reasoning backed up by concrete and convincing facts."[88]

"Unsaying His Say"

Required by church authorities to retract and to issue written apologies for his erroneous publications, Bougeant finally was allowed to return to France. It seems that, in many ways, his work is prophetic of certain aspects of evolutionary theory and modern animal rights theory. It is striking that "many who cite Darwin in effect leave out Darwin's parenthetical acknowledgment of enormous practical difference between human and animal minds" (Budiansky 1998, xv). The philosopher Ludwig Wittgenstein later asserts: "If a lion could talk, we would not understand him" (quoted in Budiansky 1998, xxii). Bougeant's audacity is that he actually, to paraphrase the *Amusement*, maintains that a lion does talk, and that it is the shortcoming of humanity that man cannot understand—or willfully refuses to hear—what the lion is saying. "If our greatest obstacle to entering the mind of another animal is its inability to communicate as we do, the second greatest is our self-centered way of looking at the world. . . . We are forever . . . invoking the metaphor of intentionality. Man's readiness to ascribe human motives and intentions to phenomena at large . . . has made us very bad at being objective about the true nature of the things in the world that are actually not like us" (Budiansky 1998, xvi–xviii). By putting the lion on a par with man—not whittling away the lion's distinctiveness by facile evocations of purportedly similar behavior, as in the strategy of anthropomorphizing, but rather asserting a noble difference between man and beast, and then by elucidating a reasoning capacity, a language, and a soul for the animal, Bougeant renders his arguments unacceptable, even anathema, to contemporary authority.

This ground for reasoning, the ground of personal experience and observation, is the centerpiece of the devotional manual. De Sales bases his appeal for the development of human spirituality on man's ability to touch, to see, to know, his propensity to experience physically and in tactile fashion the terrestrial world and, especially, the goings-on of the animals that inhabit it as our companions and our guides. Experiential reasoning parallels the Cartesian emphasis on experiment (*expérience*) but without the intellectual or protoscientific overlay or rationale; what is required, what will be sufficient, is a hands-on approach to the world. The genre of the devotional manual shows how this experiential understanding of the world could lead beyond the world to a personal and experiential encounter with metaphysical reality.

Bougeant's argument does not use that formula, nor does he develop it in the format of the devotional manual. From what we have seen of the devotional manual's status as para-ecclesial literature, it is very likely that if the *Amusement* had been a devotional manual, it would have not incurred such opposition from authorities. There are, nonetheless, similarities. Like Montaigne, and like de Sales, Bougeant uses observation and personal experience to develop his argument for animal worth, animal language, and, most boldly, animal souls.

Unlike de Sales, who is careful not to ruffle ecclesiastical feathers, Bougeant insists on developing his position from within theological parameters that are sure to threaten church authorities. And unlike de Sales, who develops his *spiritual* teaching using the *imagination*, Bougeant relies on *intellectual* reasoning and *theological* argumentation. His text has been deemed "obscure" because it was censored and not widely available. Yet interestingly enough, Bougeant has become the darling of the animal rights movement today in Great Britain.

Bougeant's thought deserves a wider hearing than it received in his own day. And animals deserve far more than that. How he was treated, and how they have been mistreated, reveal an entire ideology of opposition. As Diana Fuss has asserted, "The vigilance with which the demarcations between humans and animals . . . are watched over and safeguarded tells us much about the assailability of what they seek to preserve: an abstract notion of the human as a unified, autonomous, and unmodified subject" (1996, 3).

CONCLUSION

Faith in Fauna

How do you know but ev'ry Bird that cuts the airy way
Is an immense world of delight, clos'd by your senses five?
                    —William Blake, *The Marriage of Heaven and Hell*

The Naming of Cats is a difficult matter,
It isn't just one of your holiday games.
                    —T. S. Eliot, "Old Possum's Book of Practical Cats"

Every thing that lives is holy.
                    —William Blake, *The Marriage of Heaven and Hell*

Wise World

Over a quarter century ago, the British historian Keith Thomas, acknowledged by many as the progenitor of work on animal rights, published *Man and the Natural World: A History of the Modern Sensibility*. This book documented the *mentalité*, from the late Middle Ages through the present day, that English men and women evinced toward animals, both wild and domestic. Drawing primarily on oral tradition, such as a wealth of proverbs and folk utterances having to do with the natural world, and also from literary works and religious treatises, Thomas showed that at least a suggestion of a more enlightened attitude had emerged over the centuries, one that considered animals to have rights to fair and considerate treatment equal to man's own. These rights were predicated on a worldview initially arising in the realm of more radical strains of religious belief that asserted the divinity of all creatures, human or not (Thomas 1983, 154). He cited, for example, the words of a bricklayer named Marshall, follower of the Familists, who asserted that it was "unlawful to kill any creature that had life, because it came from God" (Thomas 1983, 291). The Ranter Jacob Bauthumley maintained stoutly that "God is in all creatures, man and beast, fish and fowl, and every green thing" (Thomas 1983, 291). This sort of new understanding, predicated on a revision of theology, in turn led to the secular view that all aspects of the environment deserved protection and had inherent value (Thomas 1983, 301).

Thomas acknowledged that his study bore a considerable indebtedness to continental thought, particularly to French philosophy and natural history and especially to the writings of Michel de Montaigne. However, Thomas admitted that a thorough exploration of those sources of thought lay beyond the scope of his endeavor (1983, 182). Such a full treatment had yet to be written at the time of the publication of *Man and the Natural World*.

Admittedly, in many respects the changes in attitudes that Thomas hoped to discern have not always held up to critical investigation. As Donna Haraway has shown, given the extensive and usually unapologetically sadistic use of animals for biological experimentation, we may have regressed. And philosophers such as Jacques Derrida represent a puzzling and persistent failure to be fully attentive to animals in terms of a radical respect for their alterity. When Derrida's cat gazes at him, Haraway suggests, Derrida could go beyond simply recognizing its alterity and actually respond to that gaze. He could practice a form of engagement with animals "that risked knowing something more about cats and *how to look back*" (1989, 20), as some ethologists have done, undertaking "the risky project of asking what this cat on this morning cared about, what these bodily postures and visual entanglements might mean and might invite, as well as reading what people who study cats have to say and delving into the developing knowledges of both cat-cat and cat-human semiotics" (1989, 22). It is, however, encouraging that recent perspectives in animal studies theory are deepening our understanding of biological continuism and undoing metaphysical separationism.

In this book I have framed the texts under examination as cultural productions demonstrating sensory experiences from the natural world, among them sight as theater or spectacle; play or ludic activity also as seen, perceived, and mirrored; and the performative visual aspect of body language, gestural speech, and even deaf-mute signing. The primary visual metaphor is that of "visive violence," appropriate to the ideologies and theologies manifested in the texts' discussion of species and interspecies relationships, as *specere* means "to look" or "to behold," and "in logic 'species' refers to a mental impression or idea, strengthening the notion that "thinking and seeing are clones"—a mentality that at least some of these texts seek to bypass (Haraway 1989, 17).

Montaigne's assessment of the rights and worth of the animal world was consistent with, and probably derived from, his proto-relativistic stance toward other cultures, such as the anthropophagous peoples in "Des cannibales." The criterion seems to be that of feeling—personal feeling, physical sensation, moral revulsion or approval. In this way, Montaigne allowed the self, its sensations and inclinations, to function as the arbiter in this ethical discussion. If the self could feel pain, and was appalled to view suffering of an animal, then that animal probably suffered, too, he reasoned, in a proleptic response to Descartes's automata argument.

Montaigne denounced cruelty to animals, partly because they shared some qualities with men and partly because they were God's creatures worthy of respect, but also because such cruelty offended his innate sensibilities: "If I see but a chicken's neck pulled off or a pig sticked, I cannot choose but grieve; and I cannot well endure a silly dew-bedabbled hare to groan when she is seized upon by the hounds" (1603, 173).

So, if the animal provides a vehicle for knowledge and a way of concretizing that knowledge in the *Essais*, the noetic impulse is recognized to be beneficial to both man and animal. In some sort of positive circular reasoning, the animal Montaigne uses to illustrate and represent his argument is also elevated and upheld by virtue of having been employed in this way. The animal's presence in the text protects both itself and Montaigne, who has reached a higher state of cognition by way of this creature. The *Essais*, famously construed as Montaigne's self-portrait, thereby offer a paradigm of the reasoned approach to all of creation: a microcosmic portrait of the world in which the text is the privileged zone, the *locus amoenus*, that allows a space for creatureliness.

Du Bartas's *La sepmaine*, a compendium of divine creation, attests at times to the surprising completeness and even commendability of the natural world over human existence. While Du Bartas, as a devout Calvinist, still upholds the dominion theory of man's dominance over creatures and describes this relationship in specular terms of visual domination, he does admit of some openings for a new understanding of human-animal interaction. He sees the world as marked by Adam's fall, a customary interpretation for a Protestant, but he also seems to suggest that God has created this glorious and various animal kingdom so as to represent back to humanity what it has forgotten: its collective self before the Fall. He further suggests that, in so representing, animals become guides and prototypes for a restored creation.[1] The self-sufficiency of different species calls humanity to similarly regulate itself and its relations with others. At a time when the Wars of Religion were raging, this was an unusual and intriguing model to pose for the cessation of hostilities and the reestablishing of a healthy nation-state along the lines of the *discordia concors* observed in nature.

That Montaigne could speak of and seek to shape the "self" in an era when such self-consciousness was only beginning to find textual expression; that Du Bartas could elevate the natural world to a status equal to scriptural loci as his chosen subject matter at a time when religious writers were cautioned not to stray from biblical truths and to eschew fiction; that Ronsard could go beyond the standard prophetic and Delphic forms purveyed by mythology and the muses to sing his own voice through animal utterance—these forays into otherness show the capacity of the animal kingdom to unleash a creative subjectivity without precedent in early modern France, and one that would have long-lasting implications for the Western world. Where France is concerned, such writing prepares the way for the whole-scale attack that seventeenth-century *libertins* mounted on the notion of man's "imaginary sovereignty" over other creatures and continues in direct line of influence to the present. As Peter Singer has observed, no one between Porphyry in the third century and Montaigne in the sixteenth century condemned cruelty to animals in and of itself (1975, 4), and the fact that Montaigne did so condemn it significantly informs Singer's activist positions.

The Renaissance/Rationalism Rift

It is so easy to forget that late sixteenth-century Protestants were really only fledgling Protestants. Up until very recently, they had been Catholics. Disagreeing with abuses of papal authority or with corrupt clergy, they invoked the authority of scripture alone. But in leaving the Catholic Church they also took much with them. Much of their mind-set even as new Protestants was retained from their mind-set as Catholics. For example, both Luther and Calvin, following Augustine's theory of "accommodation," believed, as did most Roman Catholics, that scripture and the Book of Nature were twin sources of authority. Nature was marked with God's fingerprints. For instance, herbal gardens held remedies for illness in the world, and many medicinal plants contained something in their form that imitated the malady they could cure. Similarly, it was felt that the animal kingdom had been created diverse by God and that in it could be discerned lessons implanted by the Creator from which humans could learn, a sort of animal alphabet of grace.

The split between Renaissance mind-sets such as the one just described and emerging rationalism was caused in part by the trauma of the Wars of Religion during the Reformation in France. This schism had many unfortunate effects. Much has been written about how the atrocities of this civil war pitted father against son, brother against brother, Protestant Frenchman against Catholic Frenchman, tearing apart the social fabric.

Further, there was an ideological cleavage. A fundamental alteration in worldview occurred, a paradigm shift in the way of perceiving the world and authority. Whereas during the Middle Ages and

Renaissance Aquinas had stipulated ways in which doctrine might be illustrated by the Book of Nature, now Jesuits set out to codify what was normative for the Catholic faith.[2] At the same time, Calvinists like Pierre Ramus began to draw up lists and charts—ramifications— of what was proper to know and believe. It is no accident that the upheaval of the Wars of Religion was followed by the great age of the drafting of catechetical manuals, the rote retention of what and what not to believe, and a mechanization of how to express belief. The post-Tridentine twin straitjackets of orthodoxy and orthopraxy combined to shut down this avenue of revelation. Nonetheless, this era was also one in which a para-literary form, the new genre of devotional litera-ture, also flourished, providing more leeway for spiritual perspective and extraecclesial interpretation.

Animals and nature had been jettisoned as sure and safe sources of authority. While in the sixteenth century writers had used animals in a descriptive way and in a prescriptive format, now, in the seven-teenth century, they began to use animals in a proscriptive way and in a dogmatic format. Animals were no longer there to teach man about their different experiences and delightful diversity; rather, they were symbols of man's various social behaviors and political machinations. The world of animalisms shrank to the measure of what humans knew and perceived rather than instigating the wonder to be absorbed from a formerly enchanted universe.

This paradigm shift—when the searchlight of emergent moder-nity blinded out the vast possibilities of animal diversity, difference, and ability to stipulate authoritative lessons to humanity—dimin-ished animals to mere functionaries, truncated totemic forms for man's discussion of the human condition. Cartesianism is the extreme manifestation of this result, in the scientific domain, of the hierarchical, theological mind-set of Aquinas.

This shift is paralleled in theological and philosophical thought, not simply exemplified in artistic productions or literature. Natural theology now became theology not about nature but about man. It became an anthropology rather than an epistemological possibility. After the Wars of Religion, a radical alteration in the way people thought and in the sources they accepted as authoritative often pro-duced a demythologizing of animals and of nature.

The Science of Prayer

The Protestant/Catholic divergence occurs quite significantly and extensively at this time in the realm of the approach to nature and especially to animals. Further, there is a separation of ways within Roman Catholicism itself, in which increasingly not the doctrinal texts but the *spiritual literature* (perhaps because it is conventionally less bound by dogma and more open to a personalistic expression of belief) evokes a holistic environmental and noetic unity, a shared soul among humans and animals. The writers of this literature begin to seek to discern the *imago Dei* in the *anima mundi*.

Paradoxically, animal references in Catholic writings become more numerous and more prominent as the era of scientific certainty progresses—and, in some respects, perhaps protoscience can be thanked for this, as it impels religious writers to look at the natural world afresh and in a new, detailed way, to interrogate the significance of animals' actions and to devise a spiritual understanding of a new relationship among all creatures, including man. They begin, perhaps, even to intuit the notion of a Cosmic Christ who offers salvation to all creatures and not just, as Thomist theology would have it, to the rational.

By the seventeenth century, the contributions of sixteenth-century figures to a new understanding of animals and authority evolved into a reaction to Cartesianism, a religious response to rationalism. Instead of advocating the use of animals for protoscientific experimentation, several Roman Catholic writers, most of them trained by Jesuits and many of them themselves Jesuits, began to recommend that humans' experience of the animal be incorporated into a new kind of meditational genre called the devotional manual.

The devotional manual can be seen as a parallel to, but also a religious response to, the Cartesian emphasis on method. In the *Discours de la méthode*, Descartes offered himself as authority, his own experience as test case for what he could know. He then enumerated a process to be followed in validating the truth of any matter, and this inaugurated the scientific method. But many religious writers did not want to do away with the traditional and preeminent "wisdom literature" of theology. Taking theology out of the domain of dogma and doctrine, they, like Descartes, valued individual experience in the spiritual quest, and they also delineated steps to be taken to achieve spiritual progress. These devotional manuals might be seen to imitate aspects of the Cartesian method or manual; they significantly inflect method to experiment with the cultivation of an experiential and affective spirituality.

The new genre may be seen as a sort of "science of prayer," in the sense that these writers—St. Ignatius Loyola, then St. François de Sales, his continuators, and others—aim to teach others how to pray, the process to follow in order to enter into the presence of God. In this revision of religious authority, writers use animals and the activity of animals as unmediated aspects of creation that, when properly understood and applied, may point toward the Creator. In the devotional manual, animals are employed not for scientific dissection but for spiritual direction.

In fact, a new theology may actually have been developing in tandem with the new focus on spirituality. One of St. François de Sales's continuators, Pierre de Bérulle, in his very Christocentric theology, insists that the role of the Incarnation is to restore humanity. He states that humans are destined for grace, that by their very nature, because they are fallen, God will raise them up through grace. However, the implication is that since animals have not sinned and have no need of such restoration they are more pure and untrammeled and may function as privileged conduits for the working of grace in humans' lives; animals thereby assist in the divine act of restoration. This assertion forms an interesting parallel to Bougeant's assertion that animals are not sinful—that their demonic souls are infused from sinful humans but that the sin is neither the responsibility nor the attribute of the animal.

Prelapsarian animals had language, just as did human creatures, and these idioms were mutually comprehensible (as evidenced, for instance, by the serpent's voiced temptation of Eve). One penalty of the Fall was the loss, not only of man's ability to walk in the garden and speak intimately with God, but also of his ability to understand the speech of animals. For Du Bartas, postlapsarian humanity must be restored to communion with God and with animals, through the medium of animals. This would be the understanding of dominion theology: the loss of communication with animals is a penalty rather than a sign of man's superiority. Dominion theology is thus shown to represent a cutting off of communication, a rift in relationality.

Cartesianism sought to effect a schism between theology and science, to say that science was the new wisdom literature to the extent that it dealt with life-and-death issues. For creatures (erroneously) deemed inferior to humanity, Cartesianism would be a black theology indeed. However, for most contemporary Roman Catholic authorities, Cartesianism was acceptable. Orthodoxy upheld and concurred with Descartes's claims—derived from Thomist theology—based on man's superiority to animals. Only the radical few such as those whom this study examines, dissented, and some paid dearly for it. Cartesianism then seems a form of dominion theory writ large that asserts: man is superior to animals because of reason and language; therefore he can do to them whatever he likes. Contemporary spiritual writers, however, actively combated the error of this hypothesis.

Fauna and Faith: Protestant and Catholic Interpretations

In general, what emerges from our inquiry into the relationships between animals and authority in the early modern era may be schematized in the following way. Protestants tend to rationalize their use of animals, while Roman Catholics instrumentalize their application. The uses are linked to the two faiths' divergent understandings of soteriology. That is, where salvation is concerned, a Calvinist would conclude that all we can do is know, we cannot change our state, while a Catholic would assert, in what has been (pejoratively) termed "works righteousness," that we can use what we know, we can improve our status.

Consequently, for a Protestant the application is generally purely descriptive, whereas for a Catholic doctrine may turn out, as was certainly the case for Bougeant and de Sales, to be insufficient. Protestants allowed the animal to remain at the level of imagery— exquisitely detailed imagery, admittedly, in the case of Du Bartas, but imagery nonetheless. Catholics found a way to circumvent or augment authority, using animals as a vehicle, using the physical domain to open up entry into the metaphysical realm. The focal point through which de Sales accomplishes this is action and motion: the animal is characterized, not by its physical description, but rather by its habits and habitual activities, such as the hiving of a bee.

While Bougeant differs from de Sales in many ways, most notably in his choice of genre (had he written a devotional manual, he might not have been brought up on charges of heresy), when he uses theological terminology and argumentation he introduces a concept new to the West: the notion that animals possess souls—albeit "demonic" souls, which, in his cosmogony, are "infused" into the animal from sinful human souls. In that way, he makes humans responsible for evil intentionality in the universe and exonerates creatures. Such new ways of thinking about, and expressing, man's relationship to other animals create new theological understandings that get worked out in these texts.

Diarmaid MacCulloch has argued that the signal difference between Reformation Calvinists and the Catholic Reformation was not, as has often been asserted, the schism between reliance on Word and reliance on image but rather the split between image and gesture (MacCulloch 2009, 566). By this MacCulloch means that Protestants read the Word in printed form, thereby potentially reifying it as static image on the page, whereas baroque Catholic Reformation orders such as the Jesuits had great success because they relied on drama, theater, and gestures of the liturgy to evoke a response through movement. The synesthetic approach to animals found in Bougeant and, especially, in de Sales and his emphasis on characteristic animal activities rather than attributes uses the senses to construct a dynamism in which animal and authority confront and inflect each other.

This theology of creatureliness is ultimately a protoscience of the imagination. The critic Krzystof Pomain argues that curiosity, theology, and science are all distinct categories—but in *this* theology of creatureliness, we see these categories conjoining and cooperating (cited in Findlen 1994, 94). Writers such as Bougeant and de Sales find a way to recuperate the "I Am" of God from the reductive rationalism of Descartes's "I think, therefore I am." Animals offer the way through and past the intellect and the confines of ratiocination to offer a unitive and mystical path to metaphysical understanding and awareness.

In his quintessential work relating animals and authority, for example, de Sales asks, "*How* do I know what I know?" His animals are emblematic of a *process,* not static affirmations. Montaigne's playful cat, teasing and playing with the owner rather than the reverse; Bougeant's responsive dog; de Sales's cunning and resourceful wolves hunting a stag—these are all creatures questioning authority, moving us in and through terrestrial experience and opening up new, vibrant, ways of experiencing both this world and that beyond it.

Anthropomorphizing Authority

Although the ethologist Jonathan Balcombe identifies the eighteenth and nineteenth centuries—that is, the era of Enlightenment rationalism—as the time in which an awareness of animal issues and concerns for animal welfare began to come to the fore, we now realize that there is a considerable backstory (Balcombe 2010, 14). Indeed, as we have seen, during the late sixteenth century and throughout the seventeenth, Western civilization began to grapple with matters concerning animals. And while the ideological and determinative obstacle at which Balcombe tilts is science, we find that its predecessor "wisdom literature," theology, was a formidable source of authority that needed to be confronted in the early modern era.

Today we term other creatures "nonhuman animals." The failure of both Cartesian science and Kantian cosmopolitanism to bridge the reason/instinct, human/nature divide means that legal definitions of "person" inevitably and perhaps even intentionally exclude animals (Northcutt 2007). So the term *nonhuman animal* reminds us that we are all creatures on this earth and, as le père Bougeant argued, equally—if differently—intentional, communicative, and socially bonded. And we are all not merely enfleshed, as Du Bartas beautifully illustrated in his compendium—a necessary first step—but also, the quantum leap, *ensouled*. As de Sales taught us, the activities of animals can call us to a deeper and higher awareness of our realities, both physical and spiritual. De Sales, in fact, gestures toward what Michael Northcutt has deemed a necessary and "more situated account of consciousness," and Bougeant, in his discussion of animal language, and societies, seems to anticipate what philosopher and anthropologist Bruno Latour highlights as the role of intentionality in nonhuman persons.[3] Feminists like Martha Nussbaum (1998, 559) call for the reinstatement of narrative and the "ethics of care" emphasizing context and relationality; just so, le père Bougeant insists, expanding to some extent on Montaigne, many animals are social and political creatures, possess altruism, and can and do communicate. And the present-day philosopher Christine Korsgaard concurs, in ways not so very different from those adopted by some of the early modern figures we have examined here. She speaks of "moral animals"—by which she means both human and nonhuman—and rejects the separation of the categories "animal" and "person," deeming us all "fellow creatures" in the moral enterprise (2012, 2004).

We find that the inevitable consequence of a lived, compassionate theology of creatureliness in Du Bartas's context of civil wars, and also in what has been called the "most religious," hypertheological—even as early science was developing—seventeenth century, is an awareness that voice and agency have been denied to animals at the highest levels of social, religious, and cultural power (Brémond 1936, 199). They may at times have been *spoken for*, but they have not been permitted to speak. "The problem in our relationship with animals is that our treatment of them hasn't evolved to keep up with our knowledge. . . . Animals' position relative to a sphere of moral consequence remains unchanged: they are outside it" (Balcombe 2010, 14). Thus "person" in the theological sense has given all privilege to humanity. Personhood, however, through le père Bougeant's daring and even heretical statement about language and soul, and through de Sales's daily-life applications of animal habits and activities as normative for healthy human existence and directive of a salubrious spirituality, begins to be a valid construct; these authors begin, against authority, to describe animals as "persons," not just as figures in an enumeration of creation.

Animal Eschaton

The wolf will live with the lamb,
The leopard will lie down with the goat,
The calf and the lion and the yearling together;
And a little child will lead them.
The cow will feed with the bear,
Their young will lie down together,
And the lion will eat straw like the ox.
The infant will play near the hole of the cobra,
And the young child put his hand into the viper's nest.
They will neither harm nor destroy on all my holy mountain
For the earth will be full of the knowledge of the Lord.

—Isaiah 11: 6–9

There is hope on God's holy mountain. In *Hope for Animals and Their World*, Jane Goodall says the hope for animals and for the world lies in an ethics of love and a politics of relationship. Both of these attitudes, and suggestions for how they might be practiced, we already find in the early modern works of Jesuits and Salesians. The notion of the progressive divinization of creation, termed theosis, is found in Western theology in the writing, for instance, of the modern Jesuit Karl Rahner: all humanity is called to a co-participation in the nature of Christ, a progressive in-spiritation and indwelling by God, and this can be progressively achieved through the free gift of grace.[4] But those who conceive of a Cosmic Christ, such as Andrew Linzey, take the further, final, necessary (in my opinion) step: Why would God leave this offer untendered to the rest of his creatures? Linzey argues that man's relationship to animals should be analogous to that of Christ to man: he intercedes to obtain salvation for them (Linzey's concept of "generosity"; 1988, x). This theological next step seems profiled in the theology of creatureliness developed in the texts examined in this volume. Indeed, in the case of de Sales, there seems to be a reversal of the traditional hierarchy that Linzey's thesis would nonetheless still maintain, for de Sales suggests that animals intercede for man as forms of spiritual guides. The emphasis is on participation, relationship, mutuality on the spiritual path.

French writers and thinkers of the early modern period worked creatively in applying attitudes of anthropocentrism to *animalia*. The real area that has not been much worked is that of the intersection among theology, theological anthropology, animal studies, and literature. It is hoped that this present volume has in some measure remedied that lack. We call these creatures our "companion animals," but we have yet to fully realize the significance and the moral freight of that term. "Cum panis" is Latin for "with bread"; this book has tried to develop a more sacramental—indeed Eucharistic (with bread)— understanding of a variety of approaches to animals and spirituality in the early modern era. Authority is surpassed as a theology of creatureliness is developed. Aquinas's dictum that "grace builds on nature," so relentlessly defined as "human nature," becomes here, in this era, in these texts, more capacious, more inclusive.

NOTES

Introduction

The first epigraph is from Bacon (1620, 3:370); the second is from Linzey (1995, 4); the third is from Fudge (2002a).

1. Works such as Peter Abelard's *Questiones naturales* summarized such animal-oriented and animal-exemplified science.

2. "The interest which wild and domestic creatures had for men of the later twelfth century, the keeping of pets, including exotic species such as apes and parrots, kept by jongleurs, and in baronial halls, as well as the courts of princes, also of the power of animals, in their capacity as symbols, to evoke the most varied, and often seemingly irrelevant, associations . . . lea[ds] both back to folklore and fable and forward to the romances of chivalry" (Klingender 1971, 353).

3. An example is French manuscripts such as those produced in workshops such as those of the artist Jean Pucelle. Animals also feature frequently in the lavish illustrations of Jean de Berry's *Très belles heures.* The thirteenth-century *Bestiaire d'amour,* penned by Richard de Fournival, introduced animals into the realm of courtly love discussions.

4. This approach is continued, but also significantly reworked, in seventeenth-century devotional literature.

5. The German moralist Johann Agricola wrote in 1528 that "Our Lord wishes people to conform to rule in external matters no less than in their thoughts. . . . If this is not done we shall become no better than beasts and irrational animals" (Hale 1994, 421).

6. "The distinction between 'wild' and 'tame' animals was at bottom religious rather than zoological, and had ancient roots . . . in the Judeo-Christian account of the creation and of *man's* fall from grace which . . . served to explain the state of war in nature. In the primal paradise garden, the newly created animals lived in a state of respectful unity with Adam and Eve. . . . Paintings of Eden by sixteenth- and seventeenth-century masters such as Rubens and Jan Brueghel represented this state. . . . However, the lions, tiger, wolves, hyenas and bears which had once gamboled harmlessly in Eden were destined to become part of God's curse on disobedient humanity . . . the beginning of a moral divide" (Donald 2007, 161).

7. For instance, Guillaume Salluste Du Bartas and Michel de Montaigne, embroiled in the horrific French Wars of Religion, related to animals in different ways to evoke what was being destroyed, what was being lost, what was passing away, in terms of man's relationship to the natural world and the animals within it, but also in reference to hostilities between humans.

8. "In the wake of the political and religious upheavals of the Reformation era that called into question other forms of authority, the 'old' no longer had the security of meaning it had formerly enjoyed. The fragmentation of Christendom and the erosion of traditional social rights and political privileges created a world within Europe that seemed potentially as strange and unpredictable as the New World. The seventeenth-century natural philosopher, creator of the new encyclopedia, searched for new models to explain a perplexing, increasingly expansive, and pluralistic universe" (Findlen 1994, 71).

9. Although this study does not engage in depth with her ideas, a certain theoretical indebtedness to the groundbreaking work of Donna Haraway must be acknowledged up front. It is to be hoped that her influence will be read, as it were, *en filigrane* in the ensuing pages.

10. Interestingly, a current belief about horses as "spirit guides," intuitively able to elicit what is hidden within us, spurring us to overcome past fears and abuse—constitutes a thorough reversal of the Cartesian model.

11. Not all of Descartes's contemporaries agreed with this view. La Fontaine, in his "Discours à Madame de la Sablière" and in many of his fables, strove to discredit it: his "ascription of thought and speech to animals in fables ran counter to the mechanistic theory of animal existence proposed by Descartes" (Donald 2007, 115). This raises the question of the perception of animals' possession of moral agency in this era. Animals were put on trial for their misbehavior in the Middle Ages and the early modern period, so clearly at least the rudiments of such a concept existed (Cohen 1986, 6–37; I am grateful to my colleague Walter Simons, chair of the Dartmouth College History Department, for this reference).

12. In *Animal Rights: A Christian Assessment* (1976), Linzey observes that until the nineteenth century man did not envision animals except as they satisfied human needs and had no concern for their moral being. During this period, Christian theologians had very little to say on the subject (although Judaism and Islam did: creatures belonged to God, and man was their steward). Linzey states that the notion of "animal protection" as one of man's duties emerged at this time. He also notes that the church, from 1956 on, began to issue position papers and "declarations concerning animals"—finally.

13. Linzey says that our treatment of children should function as the paradigm for how we treat animals. As we use our power to prevent children from suffering, we should restrict our behavior so as to shield animals from the suffering generated by humanity. He provides a rational argument for the moral consideration of animals.

14. Vivisection, animal eugenics and patenting, and experimentation all are "idolatrous" and, as abuses of God's creatures and gift, also abuses of natural law (Linzey 1976).

15. Linzey criticizes Karl Barth, for instance, for excessive anthropomorphism, yet concedes that "even Barth does recognize that creatures may have providential values we are not able to discern" (1976, 103).

16. A close reading of scripture should have led Calvin to advocate vegetarianism, Linzey points out (1976, 127).

17. The term *soul* should be clarified for the purposes of this study: the meaning of *soul* has changed since the classical and medieval periods, when having a soul simply meant being alive; Aquinas cited scripture to use "soul" as the equivalent of "living creature." But Aquinas, like most other medieval scholastics, said that animals did not possess immortal souls. For him, the human soul had certain features and characteristics that other kinds of souls did not, and it was higher in the order of creation as a result.

18. In recent years, scholars have begun to look at animal life in new and diverse ways. For some, like Harry Berger (1990, 2010), animals represent the metaphoric convolutions of textuality. In the framework of the history of ideas, Robert Lurz uses animals as media for philosophical discussion in his *Philosophy of Animal Minds* (2009). For PETA members or animal rights advocates such as Peter Singer, animals feature as the focus of activist outcry over unbridled consumerism, unethical treatment, and exploitation. Both the history and the ethical ramifications of humans' interactions with animals—and the development of ethically motivated vegetarianism—are examined in studies such as Tristam Stuart's cultural history *The Bloodless Revolution* (2006).

19. Donna Haraway's comment underscores the appropriateness of such framing, especially one that emphasizes sight: "The history of [animal studies] has been repeatedly told as a progressive clarification of sightings . . . progress from misty sight, prone to invention, to sharp-eyed quantitative knowledge" (1989, 4).

20. This is the case with "builder birds," for instance, whose architectural structures we have emulated. These similarities and perceived animal superiorities are, in part, what enables St. François de Sales to use animals as vehicles for spiritual progress.

21. Montaigne, one of the earliest known "theriophiles," or animal-esteeming philosophers, generally considered "animals [to be] *superior* to human beings in the modesty of their demands, and in their freedom from gratuitous violence, ambition, and guile" (Donald 2007, 117). Similarly, Bernard Mandeville's seventeenth-century theriophile text the *Fable of the Bees* demonstrated an urgency to rectify the injustices done to animals in the name of human dominion.

22. Rather, he uses buildings and construction, spaces—labyrinths, fences—material objects often drawn from prototechnological innovations (such as spectacles) or actions (such as the prestidigitation of jugglers or magicians). We

can contrast this austerity regarding the use of animal imagery with the prevalence of such symbolism and numerous animal anecdotes in the late medieval *Life of St. Francis*, for instance.

23. Of course, numerous other authors worked with animal imagery during this time period. Some who could be more fruitfully explored in another study will be mentioned in this present work in the notes. For example, Pierre de Ronsard, eager to "illustrate" and enhance French poetry, bejeweled his lyrics with imagery of animals, using them as metaphors for his artistic process and as decorations further adorning his poetry. His *Amours* (1572) dwelt on issues of transience and immortality, love and lust, poetic inspiration contrasted with pedantic drudgery, and the lives of both great and small through the metaphors and mannerisms of various animals. His treatment of animals raised issues of authority and authorship in primarily a secular sense.

24. De Sales's innovative use of animal imagery was partly influenced by his implementation of the technique of "Ignatian visualization."

25. His contemporary, the Jesuit writer Jean-Pierre de Caussade, extensively employed animal imagery in drafting his influential sermons, later collected under the title *L'abandon à la Providence divine*.

26. Fudge (2002a, 2); the quote is actually from the introduction to Fudge's article by *Times Higher Education*.

27. The book has received particular attention in Great Britain, where it features, along with Sir Humphrey Primatt's *A Dissertation on the Duty of Mercy and the Sin of Cruelty to Brute Animals*, on the list of progenitor texts for the Royal Society for the Prevention of Cruelty to Animals.

Chapter One. Sixteenth-Century Animal Avatars in Montaigne and His Contemporaries

For the first epigraph ("Quand je me joue à ma chatte, qui sait si elle passe son temps de moi plus que je ne fais d'elle?"), see Montaigne (1924, 2:12). For the second ("Non, mais non, mon chat, le chat qui me regarde dans la chambre ou dans la salle de bains, ce chat . . . ne vient pas ici représenter, en ambassadeur, l'immense responsabilité symbolique dont notre culture a depuis toujours chargé la gent féline. . . . Si je dis, "C'est un chat réel" qui me voit nu, c'est pour marquer son irremplaçable singularité. . . . Il vient à moi comme ce vivant irremplaçable qui entre un jour dans mon espace, en ce lieu où il a pu me rencontrer, me voir, voire me voir nu. Rien ne pourra jamais lever en moi la certitude qu'il s'agit là d'une existence rebelle à tout concept"), see Derrida (2006, 19). All French translations throughout this study are mine except for a few instances in which I cite another's published translation.

1. Haraway addresses this reproach to Jacques Derrida regarding his essay about playing with his own, postmodern cat: "Derrida failed a simple obligation

of companion species: he did not become curious about what the cat might be doing, feeling, thinking, or perhaps making available to him in looking back at him that morning. . . . He missed a possible invitation" (1989, 20).

2. "Ma balance inégale et injuste, quelle asseurance en puis-je prendre à cette fois plus qu'aux autres?" (Montaigne 1924, 2:563). Some of the arguments I am developing here are a reprise of an earlier article (Randall 2000). I also now, ten years later, find that I disagree with some of the article's conclusions, and I develop my newer perspective here as well.

3. "Les hirondelles que nous voyons au retour du printemps fureter tous les coins de nos maisons, cherchent elles sans jugement et choisissent elles sans discrétion, de mille places, celle qui leur est la plus commode à se loger? Et, en cette belle et admirable contexture de leurs bastimens, les oiseaux peuvent ils se servir plustost d'une figure quarrée que de la ronde, d'un angle obtus que d'un angle droit, sans en sçavoir les conditions et les effects?" (Montaigne 1924, 2:455).

4. "Pourquoy espessit l'araignée sa toile en un endroit et relasche en un autre? Se sert à cette heure de cette sorte de neud, tantost de celle-là, si elle n'a et déliberation, et pensement, et conclusion?" (Montaigne 1924, 2:455). Tom Conley observes that the swallow epitomizes for Montaigne a bounded form of knowing: "'Les arondelles . . .' are never described as migrating to a specific place *outside* the ken of the observer. . . . The birds merely come and leave. The bird tells us that what comes around goes around" (Conley 2011, 184).

5. "Our capacity to know is a constant quest, Montaigne tells us, repeating the term *queste* incessantly [in the *Essais*]; the end-point of that quest is within the confines of ourselves, our experience, our own room" (Randall 2000, 141).

6. There is a plethora of animal references in the *Essais*. Only a partial list follows: 1:14, 53; 1:26, 169; 1:27, 194; 1:27, 195; 1:31, 234; 1:31, 235; II:8, 75; II:12, 136; 2:12, 144; 2:12, 154; 2:30, 494; 2:30, 497; 2:8, 111; 2:8, 114; 2:2, 132; 2:12, 135; 2:12, 143; 2:12, 147; 2:12, 148; 2:12, 150; 2:12, 156; 2:12, 161; 2:12, 164; 2:12, 170; 2:12, 210; 2:12, 230 (Montaigne 1924).

7. This argument appeared in different form in Randall (2000, 137–45).

8. Bernoulli (1984, 39) speaks of his concern "de mettre la philosophie à la portée de l'homme ordinaire et de sa vie de tous les jours."

9. "Il n'a jamais en la bouche que cochers, menuisiers, savetiers, et maçons" (Montaigne 1924, 3:1037).

10. "Un style de 'chair et d'os'" (Montaigne 1924, 3:873).

11. "Mettre sur la montre" and "le face trotter" (Montaigne 1924, 1:39).

12. "Des asnes chargés de livres"; "gaver des oies" (Montaigne 1924, 1:177, 178).

13. "Si me semble raisonnable que meshuy je soustraye de la veue du monde mon importunité, et la couve à moy seul, que . . . je me recueille en ma coque comme les tortues" (Montaigne 1924, 3:982).

14. "Avec nos dents et nos griffes" (Montaigne 1924, 1:246).

15. "La conception de la justice selon Montaigne se rapproche églaement de la conception chez les Anciens. . . . Il s'agit bien d'une justice philosophique fondée sur la légitimité d'avoir des égards vis-à-vis de son semblable, mais qui ne fait pas encore appel à un corps de droits écrits. A une époque où les arguments zoophiles avaient disparu de la pensée philosophique occidentale, Montaigne constitue une exception remarquable et apparaît en ce sens comme le premier précurseur moderne du courant zoophile" (Chapouthier 1990, 113).

16. "Nous devons la justice aux hommes, et la grâce et la bénignité aux autres creatures. . . . Il y a quelque commerce entre elles et nous, et quelque obligation mutuelle" (Montaigne 1924, 2:455).

17. "La véritable autorité n'est pas donnée par un savoir accumulé, mais cette fecondité acquise d'une ouverture qui nous appelle" (Magnard and Gontier 2010, 17).

18. "Il nous faut abestir pour nous assagir" (Montaigne 1924, 2:492). This is, of course, also a play on words: *abestir* can mean "to become like an animal" or "to render stupid." "Dieu n'a-il pas *abesty* la sapience de ce monde?" (Montaigne 1924, 2:500). Again, note the double sense of *abesty*. But Montaigne has chosen this term intentionally, to elevate animal knowing over human; he could have chosen many others that would not have carried this connotation—such as *debase, bring low,* or *nullify,* far more neutral terms.

19. "Les animaux . . . des terrestres, nos compatriotes" (Montaigne 1924, 2:170).

20. Indeed, elsewhere and consistently throughout other *essais,* Montaigne speaks of animals' toleration of others' ways, as well as their ability to practice some form of religious sentiment appropriate to them: "les elephants ont quelque participation de religion" (Montaigne 1924, 2:150).

21. "Il ne nous faut gueire non plus d'offices, de règles et de loix de vivre, en nostre communauté, qu'il en faut aux grues et aux fourmis en la leur. Et ce neantmoins nous voyons qu'elles s'y conduisent tres-ordonnément sans érudition. Si l'homme estoit sage, il prendroit le vray pris de chaque chose selon qu'elle seroit la plus utile et propre à sa vie" (Montaigne 1924, 2:487).

22. "Ils luy faisoient resouvenir proprement des nids que les moineaux et les corneilles vont suspendant en France aus voustes et parois des églises que les Huguenots viennent d'y démolir" (Montaigne 1992, 79).

23. "Le bastiment et le desbastiment. . . . Quel patron et quel modèle!" (Montaigne 1924, 2:531).

24. Somewhat later scientific thinkers were equally fascinated with animal structures. See the wonderful work of French naturalist René-Antoine Ferchault de Reaumur (1683–1757) on wasps and papermaking, for instance. See also Joseph-Jerome le Français de la Lande's *L'art de faire le papier* (1761).

25. "Laissons faire un peu à la nature: elle entend mieux ses affaires que nous" (Montaigne 1924, 3:340).

26. See Gillam (2012, 70).

27. "Quoy des mains? Nous requérons, nous promettons, appellons, congédions, menaçons . . . d'une variation et multiplication à l'envy de la langue . . . Il n'est mouvement qui ne parle" (Montaigne 1924, 2:454); "En certain abbayer du chien le cheval cognoist qu'il y a de la colère; de certaine autre sienne voix il ne s'effraye point" (Montaigne 1924, 2:453).

28. "Au demeurant, nous découvrons bien évidemment que entre elles il y a une pleine et entire communication et qu'elle s'entr'entendent, non seulement celles de mesme espèce, mais aussi d'espèces diverses. . . . Aux bestes mesmes qui n'ont pas de voix, par la société d'offices que nous voyons entre elles, nous argumentons aisément quelque autre moyen de communication: leurs mouvemens discourent et traictent" (Montaigne 1924, 2:453).

29. "Ce défaut qui empêche la communication d'entre [les bestes] et nous, pourquoi n'est-il aussi bien à nous qu'à elles? C'est à deviner à qui est la faute de ne nous entendre point; car nous ne les entendons non plus qu'elles nous. Par cette même raison, elles peuvent nous estimer bestes, comme nous les en estimons" (Montaigne 1924, 2:12).

30. "Pourquoy non, tout aussi bien que nos muets disputant, argumentent et content des histoires par signes? J'en ay veu de si souples et formez à cela, qu'à la vérité ils ne leur manquoit rien à la perfection de se sçavoir faire entendre" (Montaigne 1924, 2:454).

31. "J'aymerois mieux m'entendre bien en moy qu'en Ciceron. De l'expérience que j'ay de moy, je trouve assez dequoy me faire sage" (Montaigne 1924, 3:1073).

32. "Finalement, il n'y a aucune constante existence, ny de nostre estre, ny de celuy des objets. Et nous, et nostre jugement, et toutes choses mortelles, vont coulant et roulant sans cesse" (Montaigne 1924, 2:601).

33. "Ainsin il ne se peut establir rien de certain de l'un à l'autre, et le jugeant et le jugé estans en continuelle mutation et branle" (Montaigne 1924, 2:601).

34. "Où le compass, l'esquarre et la règle sont gauches, toutes les proportions qui s'en tirent, tous les bastimens qui se dressent à nostre mesure, sont aussi necessairement manqués et defaillans" (Montaigne 1924, 2:600).

35. "Bastimens de nostre science"; "raison . . . de plomb, de cire, allongeable, ployable, et accommodable à tout biais" (Montaigne 1924, 2:588, 565).

36. "Nature . . . à nous elle nous abandonne au hazard et à la fortune, et à quester, par art, les choses neécessaires à nostre conservation; et nous refuse quant et quant les moyens de pouvoir arriver, par aucune institution et contention d'esprit, à l'industrie naturelle des bestes: de manière que leur stupidité brutale surpasse en toutes commoditez tout ce que peut nostre divine intelligence" (Montaigne 1924, 2:455).

37. See, for example, Montaigne (1924, 2:503, 514, 527).

38. See, for instance, Montaigne (1924, 2:555, 557, 567). Montaigne admits that "je ne fay qu'aller et venir: mon jugement ne tire pas toujours en avant; il flotte, il vague" (1924, 2:566).

39. "Et afin qu'on ne se moque de cette sympathie que j'ai avec [les bêtes], la théologie même nous ordonne quelque faveur en leur endroit, et, considérant qu'un même maître nous a logés en ce palais pour Son service et qu'elles sont, comme nous, de sa famille, elle a raison de nous enjoindre quelque respect et affection envers elle" (Montaigne 1924, 2:11).

40. "Bref, quelque part que j'erre, / Tant le Ciel m'y soit dous, / Ce petit coin de terre, / Me rira par-sus tous" (Jones 1970, 1).

41. "Pour Ronsard, nature et mythologie appartiennent à un même univers" (Brunel 1972, 134).

42. "Les abeilles pillottent deçà delà les fleurs, mais ells en font après le miel, qui est tout leur; ce n'est plus thym ni marjolaine: ainsi les pieces empruntées d'autrui, il les transforme et confondra pour en faire un ouvrage tout sien" (Jones 1970, 9).

43. "Belleau entend mirer la nature entière dans son oeuvre" (Schmidt 1958, 35).

44. "Si tost que tu es arrosée / Au point de jour, de la rosée, / Tu fais en l'air mille discours: / Et pendue au ciel, tu babilles / Et contes aux vents tes amours" (Ronsard 1963, 2:13–22).

45. See Ronsard (1914, 2:29–36).

46. See Ronsard (1914, 2:101–8).

47. "Cest oyseau, qui mes plaintes résonne" (Ronsard 1963, no. 117).

48. "Nous soupirons tous deux . . . / . . . / Toutefois, Rossignol, nous différons d'un point. / C'est que tu es aimé, & je ne le suis point" (Ronsard 1963, no. 117).

49. "À double aile, à muffle éléphantin, canal à tirer sang . . . ton corps d'atome, & ton nez de mastin" (Ronsard 1963, no. 60).

50. "Ah! Dit la mère [pie], en scavez-vous bien tant!" (Des Périers 1561, 533).

51. "Prophétis[ent] au laboureur" (Belleau 2005, 317).

52. "O Dieu! Quelle obligation n'avons nous à la benignité de nostre souverain Créateur pour nous avoir desniaisé nostre creance de ces vagabondes et arbitraires devotions et l'avoir *logée* sur l'eternelle base de sa saincte parole!" (Montaigne 1924, 2:579; emphasis added).

53. "Le neud qui devroit attacher nostre jugement . . . qui devroit . . . joindre [nostre âme] à nostre créateur . . . ce devroit estre un neud prenant ses repliz . . . , non pas de nos considérations, de nos raisons . . . mais d'une estreinte divine" (Montaigne 1924, 1:446).

54. "Vaut-il pas mieux demeurer en suspens que d'infrasquer en tant d'erreurs que l'humaine fantaisie a produictes? Vaut-il pas mieux suspender sa persuasion que de se mesler à [des] divisions séditieuses?" (Montaigne 1924, 2:505–6).

Chapter Two. Job's Horse and Other Creatures

The first epigraph is from the King James Version. For the second epigraph, see Calvin (1847, 1:28).

1. "Les autres pensent que j'ay recherché industrieusement plusieurs digressions et hors de propos pour faire une vaine parade de suffisance. . . . Mais je désire qu'ils soient advertis que d'orenavant j'entre en une si grande mer d'histoires que je ne puis éviter, bien que je presse mes discours, et geine mon stile, que je ne face de chacune des journées . . . quatre Livres assez grands" (Du Bartas 1981, "Appendice," 346–47).

2. "Il prend plaisir à voir" (Du Bartas 1981, 306, v. 65).

3. "[Il] rit d'aize en son courage. / Et tient toujours ses yeux collez sur son ouvrage. / Il regarde tantost par un pré sauteler / Un agneau" (Du Bartas 1981, 303, vv. 5–7).

4. "Il void ore comment la mer porte-vaisseaux / Pour homage reçoit de tous fleuves les eaux. / Il void que d'autre part le Ciel ses ondes hume" (Du Bartas 1981, 306, vv. 55–57).

5. "Son oeil, qui n'a point pour un temps autre objet" (Du Bartas 1981, 305, v. 51).

6. "De mesme l'Eternel ne bastit l'Univers / Pour les hostes des bois, des ondes, et des airs: / Ains pour celuy qui peut, *ores jettant sa veue* / Sur les regnes salez, ore sur l'estendue / De la terre . . . ore *devers les yeux*, / Qui d'un ordre sans ordre esclairent dans les cieux" (Du Bartas 1981, 270, vv. 419–24; emphasis added).

7. "L'Esprit de Dieu nous propose soudain és sainctes Escritures, tout ce monde visible, comme un grand livre de nature, et de vraye théologie naturelle, et toutes les créatures, comme des prescheurs" (Viret 1573, 1).

8. "Une collection raisonnée, significante, voire symbolique"; "fictionnalisation des animaux" (Hoffmann 2006, 185, 187).

9. "Ce principe ancestral de la lecture du monde, très vivace encore au xviie siècle" (Magnien 2006, 49).

10. "Le poète . . . a pour maxime très nécessaire en son art de ne suivre jamais pas à pas la vérité, mais le vray-semblance et le possible" (Ronsard 1914, 80–81).

11. See Adams and Yates (1997). See also Dorian (2000, 310–17). The classic study is Kaiser (1957).

12. "Dans la création telle que le concept de Du Bartas, le critique voit maintenant la création même de l'univers baroque, image éblouissante d'un 'labyrinthe sur les marges duquel grouillent les animaux . . . s'épanouissent les fleurs, vibrent de fulgurantes planètes, passent de météores sombres'" (Schmidt 1958, 235).

13. "Araignées et chenilles" (Du Bartas 1981, 334); "Quoy qu'il en soit, le chant des rossignols se fera entendre parmi l'importun craillement des corbeaux et fascheux coüassement des grenouilles" (333).

14. Most recently, with Bellenger (1993).

15. Like Gregory of Nyssa, Du Bartas asserts that, in the eyes of God, "man is beyond price." Also like Gregory, Du Bartas highlights the "supremacy" of God's mind, an "intermixture of the intellectual with the sensible world" (Gregory of Nyssa 1893, 480).

16. "Puisque . . . l'office d'un ingénieux escrivain est de marier le plaisir au proffit, qui trouvera estrange si j'ay rendu le paisage de ce tableau aussi divers que la nature mesme?" (Du Bartas 1981, 119).

17. "Je ne mets point en oeuvre des pierres fausses et contrefaites, ains des vrais diamans, rubis & esmeraudesPrises dans le sacré cabinet de l'Escriture: & . . . je contribue ce peu que Dieu m'a donné, à la structure de son saint tabernacle" (Du Bartas 1981, 354).

18. See Vickers (1988); Ong (2004).

19. Du Bartas does focus more on some animals than on others, but Bougeant, in contrast, aims to show language, communication, and the existence of soul in animals, so he is quite particular about which animals—birds, dogs, etc.—he will discuss.

20. Some other Calvinist writers evidence a much bleaker outlook: Du Bartas's friend Agrippa d'Aubigné, for example, invokes an animal metaphor to characterize the religious strife, quoting the Latin phrase *Homo homini lupus.*

21. "L'animal est encore un instrument mais il a un vrai rôle chez La Fontaine . . . 104 sont des fables animalières . . . 125 animaux différents y interviennent . . . la grande vedette étant le loup (26 fois), avant le renard, le chien, le lion, l'âne, le rat, le chat, le mouton et la souris . . . En tout, 450 apparitions de l'animal sur la scène fabulique" (Bellenger 1993, 52).

22. See the chapter on Luther, Calvin, and the use of anecdote in Randall (2007).

23. As Blair and Pantin note, "In short, every man reads God in nature in the sixteenth century, and reads him in his own way" (Bref, chacun lit Dieu dans la nature au XVIe siècle, et le lit *à sa mesure;* 2006, 266).

24. "Du Bartas est d'abord apologétique et édifiant: il vise . . . à deployer le livre du monde et à montrer qu'il a été écrit de la main de Dieu; mais la lecture détaillée des merveilles de la nature procure déjà, rien que par elle-même, une inégalable récréation" (Blair and Pantin 2006, 276).

25. Quoted in "Introduction" (Du Bartas 1981, lii).

26. "Et pour l'amour de l'homme / Il aime son ouvrage" (Du Bartas 1981, 308, v. 98).

27. "Comme en chaque corps du burin de son doy / Grave le texte sainct d'une éternelle loy" (Du Bartas 1981, 311, vv. 167–68).

28. Michel Foucault (1995) talks about the construction and significance of the "penal gaze" to reinforce power during this period. "Il void cler à minuit. / Les goufres les plus profonds / Luy sont guez de christal . . . / Son oeil . . . Descouvre la pensée avant qu'estre pensée" (Du Bartas 1981, 312, vv. 174–76).

29. "Ce grand ressort, qui fait de ce grand corps / Jouer diversement tous les petits ressorts / de . . . [cette] machine" (Du Bartas 1981, 310, vv. 145–48).

30. "Bien est vray toutefois que les choses humaines / Sans fin semblent couler tant et tant incertain" (Du Bartas 1981, 312, vv. 191–92). "Mais d'un soin plus soigneux il couvre de ses ailes/La semence d'Adam, et sur tout les fideles" (Du Bartas 1981, 315, vv. 239–40).

31. Sied-toy donc pres de moy, / Discours en ces discours, voy tout ce que je voy, / Oy ce docteur muet [le monde], Estudie en ce livre, / Qui nuict et jour ouvert t'aprendra de bien vivre" (Du Bartas 1981, 324, vv. 229–32).

32. "Afin que tant de corps soyent autant de bons maistres / Pour rendre grans docteurs ceux qui n'ont point de lettres" (Du Bartas 1981, 323, vv. 435–40).

33. "Je voy que l'Elephant . . . / Escolier studieux, il rumine à part-soy / La leçon qu'on luy baille, il revere son roy" (Du Bartas 1981, 250, vv. 25–32).

34. "Voire, si des Gregeois l'histoire en nous trompe, / Il escrit quelquesfois assez bien de sa trompe" (Du Bartas 1981, 251, vv. 37–38).

35. "Le Cheval corne-pied, soudain, ambitieux / Aime-maistre, aime-Mars. . . /. . . / Tel sans maistre et sans mors fait de soy-mesme à mont, / Se manie à pié coy, à passades, en rond, / Tel suit, non attaché" (Du Bartas 1981, 253, vv. 84–89).

36. "Pardon, bon Dieu, pardon, ce n'est pas toy Seigneur, / Qui troublas de nos ans le commencé bon-heur: / C'est nostre orgueil . . . / Avant que contre toy Adam se revoltast . . . / Il vivoit Roy d'Eden . . . / Les plus fiers animaux volontiers fleschissoyent / Leur col dessous son joug, et prompts obeissoyent" (Du Bartas 1981, 259, vv. 179–88).

37. "Sus donq rois, sus vassaux, sus cours à l'escole / De l'essaim donnemiel . . . [de] l'espervier . . . [de] la chaude passerelle" (Du Bartas 1981, 329, vv. 553–64).

38. "Peres, si vous voulez que vos sages enfans / Par leur propre bon-heur bien-heurent vos vieus ans / Mettez-les au chemin de la vertu non-feinte / Par beaux enseignemens, par exemples, et par crainte. / Ainsi l'Aigle volète autour de ses petits, / Pour aprendre à voler" (Du Bartas 1981, 330, vv. 569–73).

39. "Qui s'oppose à l'injure / Faite à ses compagnons" (Du Bartas 1981, 331, vv. 604–5).

40. "La seule araignee instruit chacun de nous" (Du Bartas 1981, 332, v. 662).

41. See Linzey and Regan (1988), especially ch. 2.

42. "Imitans la vertu / Qui jamais ne s'attaque au soldat abattu" (Du Bartas 1981, 333, vv. 236–38).

43. "Ains pour l'amour de luy tu as rendu funestes / Les Serpens aux Serpens . . . / Tu fais, ô Tout-puissant, que l'ingrate Vipère / Naissant, rompe les
flancs de sa mourante mere" (Du Bartas 1981, 260–61, vv. 185–226).

44. "Cette sensibilité poétique particulière participle du sentiment que l'on
a généralement de la nature au xviie siècle. On l'aime, mais telle qu'elle n'est
pas. Il faut l'ordonner, la maîtriser. La nature brute ne fascine pas souvent et l'on
sait bien faire le depart entre les animaux qui participant au rêve et ceux que l'on
ny'y veut pas" (Bellenger 1993, 43).

45. "Un outil vivant domestiqué pour subvenir à la vie humaine" (Bellenger
1993, 15).

46. "Motivés par la nécessité de marquer la différence de destinée entre
l'animal et l'homme, d'affirmer l'immortalité de l'âme et l'existence de Dieu"
(Delort 1984, 20).

Chapter Three. The Fauna of Faith

The first epigraph is from John of the Cross (1984), the second from Primatt
(1776, p. 5), and the third from Meister Eckhart (1909).

1. These were, for the most part, later Thomist Dominicans (Tugwell 1985,
119).

2. See seventeenth-century examples such as the *Primer, or the Office of the
Blessed Virgin Mary*, the *Key of Paradise*, and Chandler's *Garden of the Soul* (eighteenth century). In France, see the manifold and various *livres de piété de la jeune
fille*.

3. The devotional manual persisted through the nineteenth century, most
especially in terms of female education; scores of *livres de piété de la jeune fille* (the
original of which went through 268 editions by 1878), *paillettes d'or*, and *fleurs
offertes à la Vierge Marie* proliferated, particularly in the South of France, and
were circulated with papal permission. Their tone was didactic, and the goal was
the formation of the young woman religious, a sort of corseting of her natural
inclinations within the girdle of piety and faith. Occasional reference was made
to animals, but on the whole such imagery was eschewed, as the hope was to
avoid dwelling on the "animal" nature—as the more orthodox, authoritative version of Roman Catholicism construed it—of the girl (deemed to be sinful), in
order to turn her toward a more "pure" and spiritual perspective.

4. As Meister Eckhart would have it, a "sermon."

5. De Sales used as authoritative sources the Bible along with the source
he consulted most frequently, Pliny, whose thirty-seven-volume *Natural History*
was widely accepted as antiquity's encyclopedia about natural phenomena and
animals. "François de Sales semble en effet s'être délecté à la lecture des trente-
sept livres de *l'Histoire naturelle* de Pline l'Ancien, encyclopédie de la science de

l'Antiquité. La plupart de ses comparaisons en sont tirées. . . . Mais le livre le plus cité demeure la Bible" (Proton 2010, 20).

6. "J'admirais . . . comment les faucons reviennent au poing, se laissent couvrir les yeux et attacher à la perche, tandis que les hommes sont si peu dociles à la voix de Dieu" (de Sales 2010, 167).

7. "Saint François, voyant une brebis perdue au milieu d'un troupeau de chèvres: 'Regarde, dit-il à son compagnon, comme cette petite brebis va doucement au milieu de ces chèvres; ainsi Notre-Seigneur passait doux et humble au milieu des pharisiens.' Et voyant une autre fois un petit agnelet dévoré par un porc: 'Ah! Petit agneleé, dit-il en pleurant, tu représentes si bien la mort d[u] Sauveur!'" (de Sales 2010, 167).

8. "The mystery of creation because of its intimacy [with God] cannot dispense with the category of participation; that God, like the sun, imparts being through his being and is present to every being, so that now no being or form can—or may be—excluded from those which can help us to find him. . . . The creaturely understanding in its movement to absolute unity is already unifying in itself (*gnosis* as *henotike*, unifying, of the knower and the known) . . . active participation in the unifying and reconciling power of God" (Von Balthasar 1984, 170).

9. "Malheureux ceux qui détournent les creatures de leur Créateur pour les faire server au péché. Mais bienheureux ceux qui font server les creatures à la gloire du Créateur" (de Sales 2010, 168).

10. It might seem problematic to hazard cross-confessional comparisons on the basis of works drawn from very different genres. Yet these authors deliberately chose to express their theology in the particular stylistic choice they made, and we can therefore honor their genre as the vehicle they each deemed best suited to convey their particular worldview. Du Bartas did not write a devotional manual; de Sales did not write an epic poem. Yet Du Bartas discusses animals and creation and authority, and de Sales displays an approach to animals and creation and authority that can be compared and contrasted to it. Bougeant relies on theological argumentation in the rather loose and worldly format of a salon discussion. Dissimilarity in genre selection does not preclude comparison among authors; in fact, the individual genres selected tell us very much indeed about the aims and beliefs of each author.

11. *Treatise on the Love of God* 1.16 (de Sales 1884).

12. *Treatise on the Love of God* 1.16 (de Sales 1884).

13. *Treatise on the Love of God* 1.18 (de Sales 1884).

14. Many more examples of St. Francis's interactions and marvelous dealings with the animal kingdom are included in Linzey and Regan (1988).

15. Quoted in Kavanaugh's introduction to John of the Cross (1987, xxx).

16. "Ce sont bien les mêmes . . . que je présente ici, mon lecteur, mais je les présente et les dispose à ma manière, qui sera différente" (de Sales 2010, 36).

17. "De même que certaines perles vivent dans la mer sans prendre une goutte d'eau saleé . . . et que les papillons appelés pirautes volent dans les flammes sans y brûler leurs ailes, de même une âme constant et forte peut vivre dans le monde sans en prendre l'esprit" (de Sales 2010, 38).

18. "Se retirer en lui-même" (de Sales 2010, 39–40).

19. "Les petits rossignols apprennent à chanter avec les grands. Ainsi par la fréquentation des saints nous saurons mieux chanter les louanges de Dieu et mieux prier" (de Sales 2010, 175).

20. "Les évêques d'autrefois et les Pères de l'Eglise étaient au moins aussi dévoués que nous à leur charge pastorale; ils ne refusaient pas pour autant de diriger les nombreuses âmes qui recourraient à eux. . . . C'est une charge . . . de conduire les âmes individuellement, mais c'est une . . . ministère qui . . . réchauffe le Coeur" (de Sales 2010, 41).

21. "On dit que la tigresse ayant retrouvé sur le chemin l'un de ses petits que le chasseur lui a laissé pour qu'elle ne le voie pas emporter les autres, s'en charge, si gros soit-il, le ramène en sa tanière,—et qu'elle n'en est pas pour autant moins rapide à la course, bien au contraire, on la dirait allegée par l'amour naturel. Combien plus un Coeur paternal p[r]endra-t-il volontiers en charge une âme où il aura rencontré un grand désir de perfection. Il la portera dans son Coeur" (de Sales 2010, 41–42).

22. "Je conduirai ses chères brebis aux eaux salutaires de la vraie devotion" (de Sales 2010, 43).

23. "Les aigles, les colombes, les hirondelles volent souvent, rapidement, et très haut. Ainsi . . . les personnes dévotes volent dans le ciel de Dieu fréquemment, promptement, et très haut. Bref, l'authenticité de la vie spirituelle se vérifie par l'agilité et la vivacité avec lesquelles la charité opera en nous et nous par elle" (de Sales 2010, 49).

24. "Le progress spirituel se fait tres simplement dans le quotidien. . . . La vie de l'Esprit se manifeste d'après les actions. . . . Voilà pourquoi les actions très viles et très communes, par exemple balayer, essuyer la vaisselle, server à la cuisine . . . sont . . . parfaites aux yeux de Dieu. . . . Or cette simplicité réside dans une attention continuelle à Dieu" (Bérulle 2000, 299).

25. "Car comme en la création . . . il y a mélange, il y a mélange aussi en l'Incarnation. . . . [Il en] résulte un divin composé" (Bérulle 2000, 27).

26. "Texte éminement moderne, que Teilhard de Chardin aurait pu écrire" (Bérulle 2000, 207).

27. "Ce nouvel homme, qui habite la terre, est un nouveau vivant. . . . Il est un divin composé de l'être créé et incréé, l'un est déifié par l'autre. . . . Nous estimons . . . la terre . . . parce que le Fils de Dieu s'est incarné en la terre et non au ciel . . . et la terre est honorée de sa Présence, est marquée de ses pas . . . est arrosée de son sang, est honorée de ses mystères" (Bérulle, 2000, 203).

28. "Ma Philothée, unissons nos coeurs à ces esprits célestes et à ces âmes bienheureuses. Les petits rossignols apprennent à chanter avec les grands. Ainsi par la fréquentation des saints nous saurons mieux chanter les louanges de Dieu et mieux prier" (de Sales 2010, 175).

Chapter Four. Le Père Bougeant's Heresy

The first epigraph is from Budiansky (1998, 194); the second is from Bougeant (1739, 107): "Je serois même tenté d'en faire des Philosophes. . . . Tel est un de ces gros Chats barbus & bien fourrés que vous voyez tranquille dans un coin . . . sans se mettre en peine des événemens qui nous agitent . . . ? Nos Philosophes sont-ils plus sages dans l'occasion?"

1. "Soul" is understood differently in this chapter from the way in which Aristotle and Aquinas understood it, as described in preceding chapters. In the protoscientific seventeenth century, Bougeant uses "soul" to mean something more than the life force in all creatures. He asserts that animals have souls that are infused from humans who, by perversion of their will, have fallen away from God and become demonic. These souls are then added on to the basic life force of the animal in a process akin to transmigration.

2. See Thomas Aquinas, q. 96: "Of the Mastership Belonging to Man in the State of Innocence," art. 1: "Whether Adam in the State of Innocence Had Mastership over the Animals?" (Linzey and Regan 1988, 17–19).

3. See René Descartes: "By these two methods we may also recognize the difference that exists between men and brutes. . . . They cannot speak as we do . . . so as to give evidence that they think of what they say. . . . The brutes have less reason than men, . . . they have none at all" (1931/2003, 38).

4. "Descartes denies language to animals and treats them like machines. . . . Animal speech is devoid of reason, the uniquely human trait which expresses itself in words, discrete, conventional units of meaning. . . . Descartes was responding specifically to Montaigne's speculations, in the *Apology of Raymond Sebond*, that animals might speak a language that we do not understand. . . . But with Descartes, language becomes the exclusive vehicle of conscious thought. Human identity is wagered entirely on the use of words. . . . The technological world was born when animals were silenced and only poets still imagined a time 'when the beasts spoke'" (Senior 1997, 62–63).

5. "Il est un peu étonnant, à vrai dire, de voir entre Bayle et La Mettrie, un religieux répandre des idées matérialistes et sensualistes sans les corriger. Le crime de Bougeant, si c'en est un, est d'avoir propagé des heresies" (Bougeant 1739/1954, 41).

6. "Le présent nous suffit. Jouir est notre objet. / Sur l'obscur avenir rien ne nous intéresse" (Bougeant 1739/1954, xi).

7. "La qualité de raisonnables nous empêche de pretender à celle d'heureux" (*Dictionnaire des gens du monde* 1770, 286).

8. La Fontaine claimed as one of his primary sources the Eastern sage Pilpay.

9. "Ils disent donc / Que la bête est une machine, / Qu'en elle tout se fait sans choice et par resorts: / Nul sentiment, point d'âme; en elle tout est corps" (La Fontaine 1962, 250).

10. "Mainte roue y tient lieu de tout l'esprit du monde" (La Fontaine 1962, 251).

11. "La première y meut la seconde; / un troisième suit: elle sonne à la fin" (La Fontaine 1962, 251).

12. "Voici, dis-je, comment raisonne cet auteur: / 'Sur tous les animaux, enfants du Créateur, / J'ai le don de penser; et je sais que je pense'" (La Fontaine 1962, 251).

13. "Qu'on m'aille soutenir, après un tel récit / Que les bêtes n'ont point d'esprit" (La Fontaine 1962, 251).

14. "Je leur en donnerais aussi bien qu'aux enfants. / Ceux-ci pensent-ils pas dès leurs plus jeunes ans? / Quelqu'un peut donc penser ne se pouvant connaître, / Par un exemple tout égal, / J'attribuerais à l'animal, / Non point une raison selon notre manière, / Mais beaucoup plus aussi qu'un aveugle ressort" (La Fontaine 1962, 251).

15. "Je rendrais mon ouvrage / Capable de sentir, juger, rien davantage, / Et juger imparfaitement, / Sans qu'un singe jamais fît le moindre argument" (La Fontaine 1962, 250–51).

16. "La Fontaine shows no real knowledge of the behavior of animals" (Tiefenbrun 1980, 153).

17. "Animals continue to speak among themselves and to humans in the . . . Fables. [But] humans are usually rational enough to analyze any situation as a brutal rapport of force and press their tactical advantage. Their language is a means of conquest, an instrument of domination. The irony is that animals also play this linguistic game of exploitation. Throughout his work, La Fontaine continues to demonstrate the continuity between animal and human speech and reason. It is a sometimes bitter version of the old enchanted view. Animals and humans continue to talk, but both now employ the instrumental discourse of science and the hypocritical language of the court" (Senior 1997, 77).

18. "Un de ces discours que l'on hazarde sans prevue . . . sans autre dessein que d'égayer la conversation . . . une plaisanterie" (Bougeant 1739/1954, 3).

19. "Il vous plaît d'assurer que je ne l'ai point avancée au hazard: vous voulez que je la traite sérieusement, & que je vous rende compte des raisons qui m'ont persuadé"; "Que vous êtes séduisante, Madame, & que vous connoissez bien tout l'empire que vous avez sur moi!" (Bougeant 1739/1954, 2, 1).

20. "La Métempsychose, c'est-à-dire, qu'au moment de notre mort nos âmes passent dans un corps, soit d'Homme, soit de Bête pour recommencer

une nouvelle vie, & toujours ainsi successivement jusqu'à la fin des siècles; Ce systeme qui est insoutenable par rapport aux Hommes, & qui est d'ailleurs proscrit par la Religion, convient admirablement bien aux Bêtes dans le systeme que je viens de proposer" (Bougeant 1739/1954, 57).

21. "Je trouve même le moyen d'expliquer par la même voye plusieurs passages fort obscurs de l'Ecriture Sainte"; "& de résoudre de grandes difficultés ausquelles on ne répond pas bien" (Bougeant 1739/1954, 24).

22. "La Religion nous apprend que les démons ont été réprouvés du moment qu'ils ont péché, & qu'ils sont condamnés à brûler éternellement dans l'enfer" (Bougeant 1739/1954, 24).

23. "Mais l'Eglise n'a pas décidé qu'ils souffrent dès à *présent* le supplice auxquel ils sont destinés" (Bougeant 1739, 25; emphasis added).

24. "Mais l'Eglise n'a rien décidé de semblable des Démons"; "ne sait point dans l'Eglise une tradition à laquelle on soit obligé de se soumettre" (Bougeant 1739/1954, 26).

25. "J'en trouve les fondemens dans la Religion même" (Bougeant 1739/1954, 61).

26. "D'autant plus que mon sentiment n'est point absolument nouveau, & que je pourrois citer quelques Auteurs qui l'ont insinué" (Bougeant 1739/1954, 26).

27. He says that although his doctrine solves many difficulties, "D'un autre côté je ne . . . vois pas des fondemens [à ce système] assez solides pour opérer une vraie persuasion; & comme il touche d'ailleurs à des objets de Religion, je crois qu'il seroit téméraire de l'adopter sans l'aveu du moins tacite des Docteurs" (Bougeant 1739/1954, 61, 27).

28. "Dieu pour ne pas laisser inutiles tant de Légions d'Esprits réprouvés, les a répandus dans les divers espaces du monde . . . en fait des millions de Bêtes de toute espèce" (Bougeant 1739/1954, 36).

29. "C'est ce qui fait ces prodigieuses nuées de sauterelles"; "Ainsi les diables que Dieu a destinés à les animer, ne manquent jamais d'emploi ni de logement" (Bougeant 1739/1954, 59).

30. "Par ce moyen . . . je conçois sans peine comment d'une part les Démons peuvent nous tenter, & de l'autre comment les Bêtes peuvent penser, connoître, sentir & avoir une âme spirituelle, sans intéresser les Dogmes de la Religion" (Bougeant 1739/1954, 37).

31. "Il est certain que la nature ne leur a donné de connoissance que ce qui leur est utile ou nécessaire pour la conservation de l'espéce & de chaque individu" (Bougeant 1739/1954, 99).

32. "La gloire, la grandeur, les richesses, la reputation, le faste & le luxe sont des noms inconnus aux Bêtes & que vous ne troubverez pas dans le dictionnaire de leur langue"; "Dans le dictionnaire de leur langue, elles ne sçavent exprimer que leurs désirs & leurs désirs sont bornés à ce qui est purement nécessaire pour leur conservation" (Bougeant 1739/1954, 100, 101).

33. "Elles n'ont pas nos avantages, mais elles n'ont pas nos défauts"; "Ne traitez point avec lui [le Chien] de Philosophie ni de Morale; car ce seroit lui parler une langue étrangère" (Bougeant 1739/1954, 106).

34. "Quel abus d'ailleurs les Hommes ne font-ils pas de la facilité de parler que la nature leur a donnée! Que d'erreurs & de mensonges sont le sujet ordinaire de nos conversations! Que d'extravagance & de bagatelles, que de médisances & de mauvais propos" (Bougeant 1739/1954, 106).

35. "Vous me demandez donc si je crois sérieusement que les Bêtes parlent. Oui, Madame; je crois très-sérieusement que les Bêtes parlent & s'entendent entrelles tout aussi-bien que nous & quelquesfois mieux" (Bougeant 1739/1954, 4).

36. "Comme l'Homme est une âme & un corps organisé ensemble, ainsi chaque Bête est un diable uni à un corps organisé" (Bougeant 1739/1954, 50).

37. "Si vous voulez donc avoir le dictionnaire du langage des Bêtes, observez-les dans les circonstances de ces différentes passions; & comme elles n'ont communément qu'une expression pour chacune, vous aurez bien tôt composé vos dictionnaires" (Bougeant 1739/1954, 153).

38. "On ne vous verra plus que dans les bois . . . pour converser avec les Oiseaux" (Bougeant 1739/1954, 157); "Que vous aurez de plaisir quand vous serez devenüe assez habile pour . . . [comprendre] tous les secrets de leur ménage!" (157).

39. "Ensuite de ces different dictionnaires réünis, vous en ferez un polyglotte qui contiendra tous les différens languages des Bêtes" (Bougeant 1739/1954, 153).

40. "C'est qu'il faut absolument retrancher tout ce qui s'appelle phrase & construction de grammaire. . . . La raison en est toute simple: c'est que ces mots expriment des idées arbitraires & métaphysiques que les Bêtes ne sçauroient avoir" (Bougeant 1739/1954, 154).

41. "[Il faut rendre] leurs expressions par des phrases composées à notre manière"; "Car à bien prendre la chose, qu'importe que les Bêtes disent une phrase personnifiée & composée à notre maniere, pourvu qu'elles se fassent également entendre?" (Bougeant 1739/1954, 153–56).

42. "Aimons-nous les Bêtes pour elles-mêmes? Non! Absolument étrangères à la société humaine, elles ne peuvent y entrer que pour l'utilité ou l'amusement" (Bougeant 1739/1954, 39).

43. "La Religion nous en apprend la raison; cest qu'ils naissent pécheurs" (Bougeant 1739/1954, 42).

44. "Admettez mon systeme; tout est expliqué. Les âmes des Bêtes sont des Esprits rebelles qui se sont rendus coupables envers Dieu. Ce péché dans les Bêtes n'est point un péché d'origine, c'est un péché personnel qui a corrompu & perverti leur nature dans toute la substance" (Bougeant 1739/1954, 49).

45. "Cette union . . . rien ne doit plus nous étonner dans les Bêtes; elles doivent connoître & sentir comme nous connoissons & comme nous sentons; &

à en juger par ce qui se passé dans nous, elles doivent être comme nous jalouses, colères, perfidies, ingrates, interessées" (Bougeant 1739/1954, 51).

46. "Cherchons donc dans la nature même les preuves de mon opinion" (Bougeant 1739/1954, 5).

47. "Les uns vont au bois, les autres à la terre glaise que quelques-uns sont chargés d'apporter en se renversant, comme on sçait sur le dos & faisant de leur corps une espéce de tombereau que les autres tirent jusques sur le lieu où il faut l'employer. Là l'un fait l'office de maçon, l'autre celui de manoeuvre, un autre celui d'architecte" (Bougeant 1739/1954, 70–71).

48. "Avec ordre & un concert parfait"(Bougeant 1739/1954, 71).

49. "N'est-il pas evident qu'une enterprise si bien suivie & si bien exécutée, suppose nécessairement que ces animaux se parlent, & ont entr'eux un langage par lequel ils se communiquent leurs pensées? Rappellez-vous, Madame, ce qui est dit de la Tour de Babel. . . . C'est ce qui arrive à toute société qui ne s'entendra pas" (Bougeant 1739/1954, 72–73).

50. "Puisque nous . . . donn[ons] de la connoissance aux Bêtes, pourquoi leur donner un instinct inutile? Pourquoi attribuer à cet instinct inconnu ce qui peut n'être que le simple effet de leur connoissance, & puisque c'est effectivement la connoissance qui fait faire à l'Homme de semblables operations, pourquoi n'en feroit-elle pas aussi le principe dans les Bêtes?" (Bougeant 1739/1954, 78).

51. "Car s'il y a quelques Bêtes qui parlent, il faut qu'elles parlent toutes" (Bougeant 1739/1954, 81).

52. "Nous appellons une langue, qui est différente chez les Peuples différens. Il est certain que si les Bêtes parlent, ce n'est point par le moyen d'une semblable langue. Mais ne peut-on, sans ce secours, se faire bien entendre & parler véritablement?" (Bougeant 1739/1954, 90).

53. "A bien prendre la chose, le langage des Bêtes ne nous paraît[-il] si borné, que par rapport au nôtre qui est peut-être trop diffus?" (Bougeant 1739/1954, 90).

54. "Une ruse si bien concertée ne suppose-t'elle pas évidemment que les . . . loups sont convenus ensemble . . . et comment peut-on convenir ainsi ensemble sans se parler?" (Bougeant 1739/1954, 91).

55. "Concluons donc que puisque la nature, qui agit toujours avec tant de sagesse, a fait les animaux pour vivre en société, elle leur a donné tous les moyens nécessaires, & par conséquent la faculté de parler" (Bougeant 1739/1954, 91). There may be a sort of building-blocks reasoning going on here; Bougeant may be anticipating the eighteenth-century *philosophe* Pierquin de Gembloux, who asserted that the original form of human language might be found through study of the speech of animals (see Thuillier 2001).

56. "Cherchons donc dans la nature même les preuves de mon opinion" (Bougeant 1739/1954, 48).

57. "Vous avez une chienne que vous aimez & dont vous croyez être aimé. Je défie tous les Cartésiens du monde de vous persuader que votre chienne n'est qu'une machine" (Bougeant 1739/1954, 49).

58. "Voilà, précisément, si l'opinion de Descartes était vraie, quelle serait la folie de tous ceux qui croyent que leurs chiens leur sont attachés & les aiment avec connoissance et ce qu'on appelle sentiment" (Bougeant 1739/1954, 49).

59. "Conceit, imagination, coniecture, supposall, guess," are all listed in Cotgrave (1611).

60. "C'est que quand je vois quelqu'un parler, raisonner, & agir comme moi . . . je croi[s] que l'homme que je vois a dans lui-même un principe de connoissance & d'opérations tout semblable au mien. Or les Bêtes sont, par rapport à nous, dans le meme cas" (Bougeant 1739/1954, 11).

61. "Elles sont à cet égard à peu près dans le cas des Paysans de nos campagnes, des Nègres & des Sauvages de l'Amérique" (Bougeant 1739/1954, 107).

62. "Je vois un chien accourir quand je l'appelle, me caresser quand je le flatte, trembler & fuir quand je le menace, m'obéir quand je lui commande, & donner toutes les marques extérieures de divers sentiments" (Bougeant 1739/1954, 68).

63. "Concluons donc qu'[ils possèdent] par consequence la faculté de parler, quel que soit leur langage" (Bougeant 1739/1954, 78).

64. "Tout parle dans une Bête amoureuse comme dans l'Homme le plus passionné. Tout exprime sa passion, ses gestes, sa voix, tous ses mouvements" (Bougeant 1739/1954, 87).

65. "Vous ne trouverez pas [beaucoup] dans le dictionnaire de leur langue. Elles ne sçavent exprimer que leurs désirs, & leurs désirs sont bornés à ce qui est purement nécessaire pour leur conservation" (Bougeant 1739/1954, 86).

66. "Leurs désirs sont bornés à ce qui est purement nécessaire pour leur conservation" (Bougeant 1739/1954, 87).

67. "Plus ou moins parfait à proportion de leurs besoins" (Bougeant 1739/1954, 88).

68. "Vous pourrez juger par lui des languages des autres Bêtes" (Bougeant 1739/1954, 109).

69. "De que vous diriez vous meme en pareille circonstance"; "précisément ce qu'elle dit!" (Bougeant 1739/1954, 112).

70. "A bien prendre la chose, le langage des Bêtes ne nous paraît si borné, que par rapport au nôtre qui est peut-être trop diffus" (Bougeant 1739/1954, 116).

71. "On peut objecter que les Oiseaux répetent toujours la même chose, & par conséquent ne varient point leurs phrases comme je le prétends. A cela je réponds qu'outre les différences qu'il est aisé de remarquer dans le parler des Oiseaux, de vîtesse ou de lenteur, de haut et de bas, de longueur et de briéveté, il y en a vraisemblablement beaucoup d'autres que nous n'appercevons pas, faute d'entendre leur langage, mais que les Oiseaux entr'eux distinguent fort bien" (Bougeant 1739/1954, 118).

72. "Je pourrais alléguer cent faits pareils pour prouver que tous les Animaux ont dans leur commerce entr'eux une finesse de discernement qui nous échappe, & qui leur fait remarquer entr'eux des différences qui sont absolument imperceptibles pour nous" (Bougeant 1739/1954, 119).

73. "Je m'imagine qu'un Homme né sourd qui entendroit pour la première fois parler les Hommes entr'eux, se persuaderoit aussi, ne connoissant ni voyelles, ni mots, ni syllables, qu'ils diroient toujours la même chose" (Bougeant 1739/1954, 120–21).

74. "Tel est le Jugement que nous portons du ramage des Oiseaux" (Bougeant 1739/1954, 93).

75. "Nous parlons tous les jours aux Bêtes & elles nous entendent fort bien. Le berger se fait entendre de ses Moutons, les Vaches entendent tout ce que leur dit une petite paysanne, nous parlons aux Cheveaux, aux Chiens, aux Oiseaux, & ils nous entendent. Les Bêtes nous parlent aussi à leur tour, & nous les entendons" (Bougeant 1739/1954, 95).

76. "Mais comparez encore, si vous voulez, ce prétend défaut à l'avantage prétendu de nos amplifications, de nos métaphores, de nos hyperboles, de nos phrases entortillées, & vous trouverez dans les Oiseaux toujours du simple & du vrai, & dans le langage humain beaucoup de verbiage et de mensonges outrés" (Bougeant 1739/1954, 95).

77. "Le langage des Bêtes & des Oiseaux n'est point sujet à ces variations incommodes. Les Rossignols & les Serins parlent précisément le même langage qu'ils parloient *avant le deluge*" (Bougeant 1739/1954, 127; my emphasis).

78. "Le Paradis était peuplé de Bêtes qui s'entendoient entr'elles & qui parloient sensément" (Bougeant 1739/1954, 144).

79. "Car si elles s'entendoient entr'elles dans le Paradis Terrestre, & si elles parloient sensément . . . avec connoissance, à propos & conformément à leurs besoins, pourquoi auroient-elles perdu ce privilege?" (Bougeant 1739/1954, 145–46).

80. With the possible exception of the communication between the Devil/serpent and Eve, problematic because it further conflates human deception in speech with diabolic intent.

81. "Ne seroit-il pas à souhaiter . . . que les Hommes sur ce modèle établissent une langue générale qui seroit entendüe dans tout l'Univers?" (Bougeant 1739/1954, 66).

82. "Associés deux personnes absolument muettes; je défie que l'union subsiste, si elles n'ont aucun moyen de convener ensemble de leurs faits & de s'exprimer leurs besoins: deux Moineaux sans aucune espèce de langage seront dans la même impossibilité de vivre ensemble" (Bougeant 1739/1954, 83).

83. "Des mines, des gestes & des mouvemens qui font une espèce de langage très-intelligible & un supplement de l'expression vocale. . . . Ne sont-ce pas des actions parlantes?" (Bougeant 1739/1954, 128).

84. "Gardons-nous cependant . . . de nous livrer trop à nos préjugés" (Bougeant 1739/1954, 132).

85. "Pourquoi n'en pourroient-ils pas, par le moyen d'un resort equivalent à la langue & au gosier, former des vibrations & des sons . . . délicats . . . qui seroient entendus?" (Bougeant 1739/1954, 133).

86. "Tout parle dans nous quand nous voulons. . . . Imaginez . . . un people de muets. Croyez-vous qu'ils ne se feroient pas entendre les uns aux autres, & que privés de l'usage de nos mots & de nos phrases, ils n'y suppléeroient pas par des cris, par des gestes, des regards & des mines? . . . Appliquons donc cet exemple aux Bêtes. Elles n'ont point de langage; mais pourquoi n'auroient elles pas un langage?" (Bougeant 1739/1954, 137).

87. "La nature est trop semblable à elle-même dans les productions d'un même genre pour avoir mis entre les Bêtes une différence aussi essentielle que seroit celle de parler ou de ne parler pas" (Bougeant 1739/1954, 86).

88. "La raison, les loix de la nature, les faits & l'expérience concurrent à le prouver avec assez d'évidence pour [le] fixer"; "un raisonnement appuyé sur des faits sensible & palpable" (Bougeant 1739/1954, 96, 94).

Conclusion

1. This view is consistent with that of another Huguenot, the renowned potter Bernard Palissy, who sculpted majolica ware featuring diverse elements of creation, such as fish and reptiles, portraying them as signs of a restored order. Regrettably and rather ironically, Palissy cast from life—thereby killing the creatures he was modeling in ceramic. See Shell (2004, 1-40).

2. And, it should be noted, many other Roman Catholic thinkers developed their own schemas to counter those of the Jesuits.

3. See, e.g., Strum and Latour (1991).

4. See the work of Sergius Bulgakov, the Eastern Orthodox theologian whose work on theosis parallels Rahner's in time period; his trilogy *The Lamb of God* (2002b), *The Comforter* (2004), and *The Bride of the Lamb* (2002a) develops a theology of the progressive divinization of all creation.

BIBLIOGRAPHY

Acampora, R. 2008. "Zoos and Eyes: Contesting Captivity and Seeking Successor Practices." In *The Animal Ethics Reader*, ed. Susan Armstrong and Richard Botzler, 2nd ed. New York: Routledge.

Adams, James Luther, and Wilson Yates, eds. 1997. *The Grotesque in Art and Literature: Theological Reflections*. Grand Rapids, MI: Eerdmans.

Anzelewsky, Fedja. 1980. *Dürer: His Art and Life*. New York: Alpine Fine Arts Collection.

Aquinas, Thomas. 1905. *Summa contra Gentiles*. Trans. Joseph Rickaby. London: Burns and Oates.

———. 2004. *Summa theologia*. Christian Classics Ethereal Library. www.ccel.org/ccel/aquinas/summa.

Armstrong, Susan, and Richard Botzler, eds. 2008. *The Animal Ethics Reader*. 2nd ed. New York: Routledge.

'Attar, Farid al-Din. 1924. "Allegory of the Valleys." In *The Conference of the Birds: A Sufi Allegory; Being an Abridged Version of Farud-ud-din Attar's Mantiq-ut-Tayr*, trans. R. Masani. London: Oxford University Press.

Bacon, Francis. 1605. *The Advancement of Learning*. London: Luminarium.

———. 1620. *Novum organum*. In vol. 3 of *The Works of Francis Bacon*, ed. and trans. Basil Montagu, 343–433. Philadelphia: Parry and MacMillan, 1854.

Balcombe, J. 2006. *Pleasurable Kingdom: Animals and the Nature of Feeling Good*. London: Macmillan.

———. 2010. *Second Nature: The Inner Lives of Animals*. London: Macmillan.

Bekoff, M. 2007. *The Emotional Lives of Animals: A Leading Scientist Explores Animal Joy, Sorrow and Empathy—and Why They Matter*. Novato, CA: New World Library.

Belleau, Rémy. 1556/2005. *Petites inventions*. In *Anthologie de la poésie française du XVIe siècle*, ed. Jean Céard. Paris: Gallimard.

Bellenger, Yvonne. 1993. *Du Bartas et ses divines Semaines*. Paris: SEDES.

———. 1998. *Du Bartas*. Paris: Memini.

Berger, Harry. 1990. *Second World and Green World: Studies in Renaissance Fiction-Making*. Berkeley: University of California Press.

———. 2010. *Caterpillages: Reflections on Seventeenth-Century Dutch Still Life Painting*. New York: Fordham University Press.

Bernoulli, René. 1984. "De Sebond à Montaigne." In *Études Montaignistes*, ed. Claude Blum and François Moreau, 31–48. Paris: Champion.

Bérulle, Pierre de. 1995. *Les opuscules de piété*. In *Oeuvres de piété*, ed. Michel Dupuy, vol. 3 of *Oeuvres complètes*. Paris: Cerf-Oratoire de France.

———. 2000. *Dieu si grand . . . , Jésus si proche . . . .* Ed. Jean Dujardin. Paris: Cerf.

Biard, D. 1966. "La Fontaine et Du Bartas." *Studi Francesi* 7 (May-August): 279–87.

Blair, Ann, and Isabelle Pantin. 2006. "La Renaissance." In *Naissances, renaissances*, ed. Frank Lestringant and Michel Zink, vol. 1 of *Histoire de la France littéraire*, ed. Michel Prigent, 262–77. Paris: Presses universitaires françaises.

Boehrer, Bruce. 2010. *Animal Characters: Nonhuman Beings in Early Modern Literature*. Philadelphia: University of Pennsylvania Press.

Bougeant, Guillaume-Hyacinthe. 1737. *Philosophical Amusement upon the Language of Brutes*. www.animalrightshistory.org/animal-rights-library/bou-father-bougeant/language-of-brutes.htm.

———. 1739/1954. *Amusement philosophique sur le langage des bêtes*. Ed. Hester Hastings. Geneva: Droz.

Brémond, Henri. 1936. *A Literary History of Religious Thought in France from the Wars of Religion Down to Our Times*. 3 vols. London: SPCK.

Broekhuysen, A. 2012. "Miguel de Molinos and Quietism." Wisdom's Golden Rod. www.wisdomsgoldrenrod.org/publications/misc/molinos_quietism.html.

Brunel, Pierre. 1972. *Histoire de la literature française*. Paris: Bordas.

Budiansky, Stephen. 1998. *If a Lion Could Talk: Animal Intelligence and the Evolution of Consciousness*. New York: Free Press.

Bulgakov, Sergius. 2002a. *The Bride of the Lamb*. Trans. Boris Jakim. Grand Rapids, MI: Eerdmans.

———. 2002b. *The Lamb of God*. Trans. Boris Jakim. Grand Rapids, MI: Eerdmans.

———. 2004. *The Comforter*. Trans. Boris Jakim. Grand Rapids, MI: Eerdmans.

Calvin, John. 1847. *First Commentaries on the Book of Moses Called Genesis*. Vol. 1. Ed. John King. Edinburgh: Calvin Translation Society.

Campbell, Ted. 2000. *Religion Publications*. New York: Kazi Publications.

Caussade, Jean-Pierre de. 1982. *The Sacrament of the Present Moment*. Ed. Richard Foster. Trans. Kitty Muggeridge. San Francisco: HarperOne.

Cavell, Stanley, Cora Diamond, John McDowell, Ian Hacking, and Cary Wolfe, eds. 2008. *Philosophy and Animal Life*. New York: Columbia University Press.

Céard, Jean, and Louis-Georges Tin, eds. 2005. *Anthologie de la poésie française du XVIe siècle*. Paris: Gallimard.

Certeau, Michel de. 1995. *Mystic Fable: 16th and 17th Centuries.* Chicago: University of Chicago Press.

Chambers, Ross. 1991. *Room for Manoeuver: Reading the Oppositional in Narrative.* Ithaca: Cornell University Press.

Chapouthier, G. 1990. *Au bon vouloir de l'homme, l'animal.* Paris: Editions Denoël.

Cohen, Esther. 1986. "Law, Folklore, and Animal Lore." *Past and Present* 110:6–37.

Conley, Tom. 1992. *The Graphic Unconscious in Early Modern French Writing.* Cambridge: Cambridge University Press.

———. 1998. "Review Essay: A Chaos of Science." *Renaissance Quarterly* 51 (3): 934–41.

———. 2011. *An Errant Eye: Poetry and Topography in Early Modern France.* Chicago: University of Chicago Press.

Cotgrave, Randle. 1611. *Dictionnaire of the French and English Tongues.* London: Dent.

d'Aubigné, Agrippa. 1995. *Les tragiques.* Ed. Frank Lestringant. Paris: Gallimard.

Delort, Robert. 1984. *Les animaux ont une histoire.* Paris: Editions du Seuil.

Derrida, Jacques. 2006. *L'animal que donc je suis.* Paris: Galilée. Trans. David Wills as *The Animal That Therefore I Am*, Perspectives in Continental Philosophy (New York: Fordham University Press, 2008).

de Sales, François. 1960. *Selected Letters.* Trans. Elizabeth Stopp. New York: Harper and Brothers.

———. 1884. *Treatise on the Love of God.* Trans. Henry Benedict Mackey. m.ccel.org/ccel/desales/love.

———. 2010. *Introduction à la vie dévote.* Ed. Didier-Marie Proton. Paris: Cerf.

Des Périers, Bonaventure. 1561. *Nouvelles récréations et joyeux devis.* Lyon: La Monnoye.

Dictionnaire des gens du monde. 1770. 5 vols. Paris: Costard.

Donald, Diana. 2007. *Picturing Animals in Britain: 1750–1850.* New Haven: Yale University Press.

Donne, John. 2001. *The Complete Poetry and Selected Prose of John Donne.* Ed. Charles Coffin. New York: Modern Library.

Dorian, Mark. 2000. "On the Monstrous and the Grotesque." *Word and Image: A Journal of Verbal/Visual Enquiry* 16 (3): 310–17.

Du Bartas, Guillaume Salluste. 1981. *La sepmaine.* Ed. Yvonne Bellenger. Paris: Nizet.

Du Fail, Noël. 1547. *Propos rustiques.* Paris: Jean de Tournes.

Eckhart, Meister. 1909. *Sermons.* Trans. Claude Field. http://en.wikisource.org/wiki/Sermons_(Meister_Eckhart).

———. 1986. *Classics in Western Spirituality.* Ed. Bernard McGinn. New York: Paulist Press.

Ellul, Jacques. 1977. *Apocalypse: The Book of "Revelation."* New York: Seabury Press.

Findlen, Paula. 1995. *Possessing Nature: Museums, Collecting, and Scientific Culture in Early Modern Italy.* Berkeley: University of California Press.

———, ed. 2004. *Kircher: The Last Man Who Knew Everything.* London: Routledge.

Foster, Richard. 1982. Introduction to *The Sacrament of the Present Moment*, by Jean-Pierre de Caussade, ed. Richard Foster, trans. Kitty Muggeridge. San Francisco: HarperOne.

Foucault, Michel. 1995. *Discipline and Punish: The Birth of the Prison.* Trans. Alan Sheridan. New York: Vintage Books.

Fudge, Erica. 2002a. "Just a Plaything for Your Pet Cat?" *THE: Times Higher Education*, August 16.

———. 2002b. *Perceiving Animals: Humans and Beasts in Early Modern English Culture.* Chicago: University of Illinois Press.

Fuss, Diana. 1996. Introduction to *Human, All Too Human*, ed. Diana Fuss, 1–8. New York: Routledge.

Gillam, Erin. 2012. "An Introduction to Animal Communication." *Nature Education Knowledge* 3 (1): 70.

Gould, J. L., and C. G. Gould. 1994. *The Animal Mind.* New York: Scientific American Library.

———. 2007. *Animal Architects: Building and the Evolution of Intelligence.* Chicago: University of Chicago Press.

Grandin, Temple, and C. Johnson. 2005. *Animals in Translation.* Orlando, FL: Harcourt.

Gregory of Nyssa. 1893. *The Great Catechism.* In *Gregory of Nyssa: Dogmatic Treatises, Etc.*, ed. H. Wace and P. Schaff, A Select Library of Nicene and Post-Nicene Fathers of the Christian Church, 2nd ser., vol. 4. London: Parker.

Hallowell, Robert E. 1964. "The Mating Palm Trees in Du Bartas' 'Seconde sepmaine.'" *Renaissance News* 17 (2): 89–95.

Handler, Richard. 1986. "Of Cannibals and Custom: Montaigne's Cultural Relativism." *Anthropology Today* 2 (5): 12–25.

Hansell, R. 1984. *Animal Architecture.* England: Longman.

Haraway, Donna J. 1989. *Primate Visions: Gender, Race, and Nature in the World of Modern Science.* New York: Routledge.

———. 2008. *When Species Meet.* Posthumanities. Minneapolis: University of Minnesota Press.

Harrison, Peter. 1993. "Animal Souls, Metempsychosis and Theodicy in Seventeenth-Century English Thought." *Journal of the History of Philosophy* 31 (4): 519–44.

Hoffmann, George. 2006. "Le cas Montaigne." In *Naissances, renaissances*, ed. Frank Lestringant and Michel Zink, vol. 1 of *Histoire de la France littéraire*, ed. Michel Prigent, 183–93. Paris: Presses universitaires françaises.

Holmyard, Eric John. 1990. *Alchemy*. London: Dover Books.

Hugh of St. Victor. 1886. *De meditatione*. In *Les oeuvres de Hugues de Saint-Victor*, trans. J.-B. Hauréau. Paris.

John of the Cross. 1984. *The Spiritual Canticle*. Washington, DC: ICS Publications. www.catholictreasury.info/books/spiritual_canticle/index.php.

———. 1987. "The Ascent of Mt. Carmel" [1578–79]. In *John of the Cross: Selected Writings*, ed. Kieran Kavanaugh, Classics in Western Spirituality. New York: Paulist Press.

Jones, K. R. W. 1970. *Pierre de Ronsard*. New York: Twayne.

Kaiser, Wolfgang. 1957. *The Grotesque in Art and Literature*. New York: Columbia University Press.

Kepler, Johannes. 1997. *The Harmony of the World*. American Philosophical Society 209. Philadelphia: American Philosophical Society.

Kheel, Marti. 2008. "The Killing Game." In *The Animal Ethics Reader*, ed. Susan Armstrong and Richard Botzler, 2nd ed. New York: Routledge.

Klingender, Francis. 1971. *Animals in Art and Thought to the End of the Middle Ages*. London: Routledge and K. Paul.

Korsgaard, Christine. 1995. *Creating the Kingdom of Ends*. Cambridge: Cambridge University Press.

———. 2004. "Fellow Creatures: Kantian Ethics and Our Duties to Animals." In *The Tanner Lectures on Human Values*, vol. 25, ed. Grethe B. Petersen, 79–110. Salt Lake City: University of Utah Press.

———. 2012. "Moral Animals: Human Beings and the Other Animals." www.people.fas.harvard.edu/~korsgaar/CMK.MA3.pdf.

La Fontaine, Jean de. 1962. "Discours à Madame de la Sablière." In *XVIIe siècle*, ed. André Lagarde and Laurent Michard. Paris: Bordas.

Le Roy, Charles Georges. 1802. *Lettres philosophiques sur l'intelligence et la perfectibilité des animaux*. Paris.

Linzey, Andrew. 1976. *Animal Rights: A Christian Assessment*. London: SCM Press.

———. 1988. Introduction to *Animals and Christianity: A Book of Readings*, edited by Andrew Linzey and Tom Regan. New York: Crossroads.

———. 1995. *Animal Theology*. Urbana: University of Illinois Press.

———, ed. 2009a. *The Link between Animal Abuse and Human Violence*. Brighton: Brighton Publishing.

———. 2009b. *Why Animal Suffering Matters: Philosophy, Theology and Practical Ethics*. London: Oxford University Press.

Linzey, Andrew, and Tom Regan, eds. 1988. *Animals and Christianity: A Book of Readings*. New York: Crossroads.

Loyola, Ignatius. 1991. "The Spiritual Exercises." In *Ignatius of Loyola: "Spiritual Exercises" and Selected Works*, ed. George Ganss. New York: Paulist Press.

MacCulloch, Diarmaid. 2005. *The Reformation: A History*. New York: Viking.

———. 2009. *Christianity: The First Three Thousand Years*. New York: Penguin.

Mackey, Henry Benedict. 1884. Introduction to *Treatise on the Love of God*, by François de Sales, ed. and trans. Henry Benedict Mackey. m.ccel.org/ccel/desales/love.

Magnard, Pierre, and Thierry Gontier. 2010. *Montaigne*. Paris: Éditions du Cerf.

Magnien, Michel. 2006. "De l'emergence à l'illustration (xv–xvi siècles)." In *Naissances, renaissances*, ed. Frank Lestringant and Michel Zink, vol. 1 of *Histoire de la France littéraire*, ed. Michel Prigent, 36–78. Paris: Presses universitaires françaises.

Manning, A., and M. S. Dawkins. 1998. *An Introduction to Animal Behaviour*. 5th ed. Cambridge: Cambridge University Press.

McGinn, Colin. 2004. *Consciousness and Its Objects*. London: Oxford University Press.

Montaigne, Michel de. 1603. *Montaigne's Essays*. London.

———. 1924. *Les essais*. Ed. Pierre Villey. Paris: Presses universitaires de France.

Navarro-Reyes, Jesus. 2010. "Skepticism, Stoicism and Subjectivity: Reappraising Montaigne's Influence." *Contrastes: Revista Internacional de Filosofia* 15:243–60.

Northcutt, Michael. 2007. *A Moral Climate: The Ethics of Global Warming*. London: Darnton.

Nussbaum, Martha. 1998. "Morality and Emotions." In *The Routledge Encyclopedia of Philosophy*, vol. 6., ed. Edward Craig. London: Routledge.

O'Malley, John, S.J. 1993. *The First Jesuits*. Cambridge, MA: Harvard University Press.

Ong, Walter. 2004. *Orality and Literacy: The Technologizing of the Word*. London: Routledge.

Parris, S. J. 2010. *Heresy*. New York: Doubleday.

Phillips, Adam. 2002. "Plumage and Empire." *London Review of Books*, October 31.

Pouilloux, Jean-Yves. 1995. *Montaigne: L'eveil de la pensée*. Paris: Champion.

Primatt, Humphrey. 1776. *A Dissertation on the Duty of Mercy and the Sin of Cruelty to Brute Animals*. London: T. Cadell, J. Dodsley.

Proton, Didier-Marie. 2009. Introduction to *Introduction à la vie dévote*, by François de Sales. Paris: Cerf.

Randall, Catharine. 2000. "The Swallow's Nest and the Hermeneutic Quest in the *Apologie pour Raimond Sebond*." *Montaigne Studies* 12:137–45.

———. 2007. *Earthly Treasures: Material Culture in the "Heptaméron" and in Early Modern Evangelical Narrative*. Lafayette: Purdue University Press.

Rochot, Bernard, Alexandre Koyré, Georges Mongrédien, and Antoine Adam, eds. 1955. *Pierre Gassendi: 1592–1655, sa vie et son oeuvre. Journées gassendistes (avril 1953)*. Paris: Grévin.

Rock, Judith. 1996. *Terpsichore at Louis-le-Grand: Baroque Dance on the Jesuit Stage in Paris*. St. Louis: Institute of Jesuit Studies.

Rolle, Richard. 1914. *The Fire of Love*. Trans. Richard Misyn. London: Comper.

Ronsard, Pierre de. 1914. *Oeuvres complètes*. Ed. Paul Laumonnier. Paris: A. Lemaire.

———. 1963. *Les amours*. Ed. Henri Weber. Paris: Garnier.

Rostand, Edmond. 1905. *Oeuvres completes*. Paris: Lafitte.

Russell, Constance, and Anne Bell. 1996. *A Politicized Ethics of Care*. London: Routledge.

Schmidt, Albert-Marie. 1958. "La littérature humaniste à l'époque de la Renaissance." In *Encyclopédie de la Pléiade*. Paris: Gallimard.

Schnapper, Antoine. 1998. *Le géant, la tulipe et la licorne: La collection et les collectionneurs dans le XVIIe siècle*. Paris: Flammarion.

Scully, Matthew. 2003. *Dominion: The Power of Man, the Suffering of Animals, and the Call to Mercy*. New York: St. Martin's.

Senior, Matthew. 1997. "'When the Beasts Spoke': Animal Speech and Classical Reason in Descartes and La Fontaine." In *Animal Acts: Configuring the Human in Western History*, ed. Jennifer Ham and Matthew Senior, 61–84. London: Routledge.

Shell, Hanna Rose. 2004. "Casting Life, Recasting Experience: Bernard Palissy's Occupation between Maker and Nature." *Configurations* 12:1–40.

Singer, Peter. 1975. *Animal Liberation*. New York: Avon.

Soergel, Philip. 1993. *Wondrous in His Saints: Counter Reformation Propaganda*. Berkeley: University of California Press.

Strum, Shirley, and Bruno Latour. 1991. "Redefining the Social Link: From Baboons to Humans." In *Primate Politics*, ed. Glendon Schubert and Roger D. Masters, 73–86. Carbondale: Southern Illinois University Press.

Stuart, Tristam. 2006. *The Bloodless Revolution: A Cultural History of Vegetarianism from 1600 to Modern Times*. New York: W. W. Norton.

Taylor, Charles. 1989. *Sources of the Self: The Making of the Modern Identity*. Cambridge, MA: Harvard University Press.

Thomas, Keith. 1983. *Man and the Natural World: A History of the Modern Sensibility*. London: Oxford University Press.

Thuillier, Guy. 2001. *Les 'Pensées et maximes' de Pierquin de Gembloux*. Paris: Presses universitaires de France.

Tiefenbrun, Susan W. 1980. *Signs of the Hidden Semiotic Studies*. Amsterdam: Rodopi.

Trench, Charles Chenevix. 1970. *A History of Horsemanship*. New York: Doubleday.

Tugwell, Simon. 1985. *Ways of Imperfection*. Springfield, IL: Templegate.

Underhill, Evelyn. 1911. *Mysticism*. London: Dutton.

Vickers, Brian. 1988. *In Defense of Rhetoric*. New York: Oxford University Press.

Viret, Pierre. 1573. *Instruction chrestienne*. London: Veale.

Von Balthasar, Hans Urs. 1982. *The Glory of the Lord: A Theological Aesthetics*. 6 vols. San Francisco: Ignatius Press.

Williams, David. 1996. *Discourse Deformed: The Function of the Monster in Medieval Thought and Literature*. Montreal: McGill-Queens University Press.

INDEX

CATHARINE RANDALL

is senior lecturer in religion at Dartmouth College.

She is the author of a number of books, including

Black Robes and Buckskin: A Selection from the "Jesuit Relations"

and *From a Far Country: Camisards and Huguenots in the Atlantic World.*